# Book of the Heart

*A personal history of seeing*

Zoe White

THOUSAND WING PRESS
AMSTERDAM

www.thousandwingpress.com

ISBN 978-90-826257-0-7

| | |
|---|---|
| cover image: | American Magpie (detail) from a print by John James Audubon |
| cover design: | Tosca Lindeboom, www.toscalindeboom.nl |
| typesetting: | Odyssey Publishing, www.odysseypublishing.com.au |

# About the Author

Born and brought up in Enfield, North London, Zoe White began her working life as a medical secretary. She then served in the Women's Royal Naval Service for four years, after which she co-owned and managed an art gallery in North Yorkshire. As a mature student, she took her M.Theol. degree from the University of St Andrews in Scotland, and her M.Div. from the Earlham School of Religion, a Quaker seminary in the USA. She subsequently taught English as a Foreign Language in France and Belgium, where she also organized conferences and seminars for international management training companies. She has facilitated workshops, led retreats and given talks on the contemplative life in Belgium, the Netherlands and the UK. Zoe sees contemplation as a creative inquiry, which she enjoys exploring through meditation, writing and photography. She lives in the Netherlands.

for Meindert,
and for the animals who help us see

*Go into your own room and get the Upanishads out of your own Self. You are the greatest book that ever was or ever will be, the infinite depository of all that is. Until the inner teacher opens, all outside teaching is in vain. It must lead to the opening of the book of the heart . . .*

Swami Vivekananda

*Here we have spoken of the heart as a kind of book, where first the eye sees, then the mind understands, and finally the affections take delight.*

Hugh of Saint-Cher

# Contents

# Preface

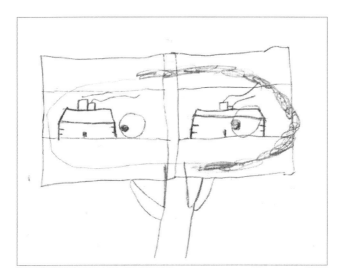

It was the last day of term. We had come to the end of the syllabus for the year and the teacher had told us to fill up the empty page in our exercise books by drawing a picture. The title of the picture was to be "At Home".

On one side of my picture, the eye is outside the house, separate and alone. On the other, the eye is inside, though the house is struggling to contain it. The windows are pushed to the side, hardly visible at all. There was no light coming in. I didn't use colour.

At first sight, it looks as though there are only two alternatives, being shut in or being shut out. The whole composition is top-heavy and I was hard-pressed (the imprint of my pencil lines can still be seen in the book four pages after the picture). A dilemma apparently had to be solved and the stakes were high.

There is, however, another view. The two houses are being looked at from a third perspective, as if through a stereoscopic viewer. I was in the middle of trying to draw this when the teacher told us to stop. I didn't know how to draw the viewer, but it was one of my favourite toys. I played with it often and I knew that when a double image was inserted into it and it was held up to the eyes, the scene became three-dimensional. People, buildings and trees appeared—as if by magic—to be standing up in space. The process of transformation from the two flat images to one three-dimensional image fascinated me. This is what I was trying to show in my drawing. This was my way of picturing home.

Apparently I knew, albeit unconsciously, that home was not synonymous with house. The home I was trying to show involved more than walls and a roof. Being at home apparently involved making shifts in seeing. Home involved at least three different perspectives, all of which could be going on, and indeed *were* going on all at once.

*Seeing* was apparently central to the way I made sense of my world. Instinctively I turned to images of the eye to help me solve contradictions which otherwise threatened to be overwhelming.

It is also clear that I was not worrying about anything. I may have been in a fix, struggling with intangibles way beyond my years, but there was no "problem". It was a puzzle and I was just playing. I was simply doing what all children do: using the materials at hand, putting down on paper what was clearly in the mind's eye, and making huge leaps of imagination.

I wonder now about the resources I drew on. What was powering my explorations and endeavours back then? Concentration, intuition, determination, and desperation probably all played a role; but there is something else, another element in the picture which could easily be missed. Smoke is the signal; there is fire in the home. To miss the smoke is to miss the fire, and to miss the fire is to be blind to the enormous passion igniting and fuelling the creative process.

The art I was practising all those years ago was contemplation. This art is my natural habitat; my way of being At Home, and whatever else I may *think* I've been doing with my life since I was seven, this is the art which has always been absorbing me.

# I

# Preview

*My eye kept telling me, "Something is missing from
all I see". So it went in search of a cure.*

Rabia of Basra, *Love Poems from God*
(trans. Daniel Ladinsky)

This is the place where two oceans meet. I'm warned in the dream
to watch out for cross-currents, which run full and fast here, but
despite the warning, I plunge into the waves for a swim.

After a few minutes I turn round, expecting to see the beach
behind me, but there's no land in sight. Fear and panic arise; this
doesn't look good. But then I notice that my body is simply floating
and I'm not frightened at all. In fact my body seems quite comfortable, not even remotely concerned. Then I look up again. This time
I can see land. It's not the beach I've just left, but there are definitely
some trees in the distance. OK, that's not too far, I can manage to
swim there. I don't know what land it is, or what country I'll find
myself in; I'll just have to see when I get there.

So here we are. Some of us floating, some of us floundering, and
some of us just dipping our toes in. The mixing and merging of the
two oceans of eastern and western spiritual traditions over the past
hundred years gave rise to a spiritual swirl, which, for some of us, was

as disorienting as it was liberating, as threatening as it was refreshing. This book arises from the maelstrom and the cross-currents.

Castes, creeds, cells and disciplines may no longer be relied upon to stay in place as they once did. Reference points, harbours, buoys and lighthouses may have been washed away, but is there a way of being at one with it all? Is there perhaps a kind of intelligence at work in the ebb and flow—another kind of knowing, which can help us swim with the swell and come to peace?

These were some of the questions which accompanied me as I bobbed about in the waves, navigated the spiritual slipstreams and swam for shore.

*

Growing up in the suburbs of North London in the 1950s and '60s, of course I knew nothing of these two oceans. Vera Lynn and Humphrey Bogart were household names and Fred Astaire and Ginger Rogers regularly danced their way across our television screen. The war had ended only a few years before my birth, and although it had never existed for me, my parents' stories of their time in the Royal Air Force before their marriage kept the ghost of it lingering. It was clear that conditions had been bleak—marches along lonely coastal promenades in freezing rain; watch-keeping in dark, muddy fields to guide planes back to base after bombing missions. But there was laughter and wistfulness in my mother's voice when she spoke the names of her wartime friends and there was no doubt in my mind that she had been happy back then.

So it wasn't surprising, perhaps, that when one of the ex-pupils of my secondary school came to give a talk on her life in the Women's Royal Naval Service it opened up a promising career possibility. Although women didn't go to sea at that time, the Navy nevertheless offered the prospect of independence, travel and training, along with the company and camaraderie I'd missed while growing up as an only child. And when my secretarial jobs in London failed to lead to anything quite so exciting, I decided to join up. After completing the initial four-year contract, I was encouraged to think about applying for a commission, and although I was flattered and tempted, by this time I wanted to explore other attractions, which had to do with the soul.

Religion had been important to me all through my childhood and ever since adolescence I'd been attracted to the religious life, but since I wasn't a Roman Catholic I thought that becoming a nun wasn't an option for me. During my twenties, however, I discovered that such things as Anglican convents did, in fact, exist. So when, having left the WRNS and worked for another two years in London as a production assistant for a touring theatre company, I found that the religious life was still drawing me, I decided it was time to give it a try.

On the surface, the decision to join a convent may appear to be a conventional one. For me, however, it was actually far more radical than the decision to join the Navy had been. The choice of the Navy was determined very much by conditioning. The convent, on the other hand, given that my family was not Roman Catholic, could not have been further from family expectations or cultural conditioning.

As it happened, my first few months at the convent coincided with the experience of meeting and falling in love with someone, which made it rather clear that a life of enclosure and celibacy was perhaps not what I was called to after all. However, although my convent career lasted only a few months, my time there was one of the richest and most significant periods of my life, not least because it was at the convent that I began to read and to study. Not only did it open up a world of learning to me for the first time; the convent also introduced me to people who were great explorers of the spiritual life, people who had made brave choices for themselves, and who were to remain an inspiration to me for many years to come.

It was at the convent that I began to realize that my comprehensive school, while good in its own way, had never been able to supply me with the learning for which I was now hungry. So, after leaving the convent, I decided to study, by correspondence course, for the A-levels I'd never got at school, and two years later, at the age of twenty-seven, I was accepted to study theology at St Andrews University. It was another break with conditioning. As far as my family was concerned, university was as unknown a world as that of the convent.

After a degree in theology and further studies at a Quaker seminary in the USA, a career in religion would have seemed the obvious path to follow. But I found that nothing was drawing me to serve as a minister in a church or to be a representative of any religious institution. The only thing which was clear on returning to Europe from America was that I should go and live on the Continent and learn languages. First I worked for The Quaker Council for European Affairs in Brussels, organising study tours for Quakers who wanted to learn more about the European political institutions in Brussels and Strasbourg. Following this, I spent five years teaching English as a Foreign Language in France and Belgium, which, in turn, led to some further years organizing courses and conferences for an international management training company.

Through all these years the spiritual life was never forgotten. One of the courses I had followed while in the USA was with the Shalem Institute for Spiritual Formation. It had prepared me to lead groups and retreats in contemplative prayer and this was something I now enjoyed doing alongside my other work. It was while leading a weekend at a retreat centre in the Netherlands that I met a Dutchman and, at the age of forty-nine, decided to move from Brussels to live with him in Amsterdam.

Although the retreat work was successful and initially when I moved to the Netherlands I was being encouraged to do more of it, I felt that I wasn't in contact with the root or the source of it and that therefore it wasn't sustainable in the long term. I also came to realize that though I had left the idea of a religious vocation behind, the mystery of contemplation still enticed me. My move to Amsterdam opened the opportunity to dive more deeply into that mystery, and this book emerges as a result of that exploration.

*

At first of course, I didn't know I was writing a book. Writing had always come naturally to me; it was simply one of my ways of exploring experience. I just enjoyed walking around, looking at things, and sketching with words what occurred to me.

I drew inspiration from childhood memories. I wrote about the church in Enfield where I had sung in the choir, the day of my confirmation and a family holiday in France. Later on, I wrote down dreams or reflections which arose during Meeting for Worship with the Quakers, or during Zen meditation. Writing was my way of savouring, processing and wondering about life. I didn't begin *seriously* to write until I got desperate.

When I moved to the Netherlands from Belgium, which had been my home for the previous ten years, I knew that Meindert was the right person for me to be living with, and that Amsterdam was the right place, but I had underestimated how disorienting and exhausting would be the combination of culture shock, starting a new relationship and learning a new language.

At first I was confident that work would turn up. I had never had trouble finding a job, but I was now just over fifty, the Netherlands had entered an economic down-turn, unemployment was rising, and my prospects of finding work were diminishing by the day. I had left an established life and a well-paid job in Belgium, so the idea of being financially dependent and "economically inactive" horrified me and I was certainly not ready to retire. I panicked and I floundered, I even enquired at the local supermarket if they needed shelf-stackers. They didn't. The Dutch course ended and the small amount of English teaching work I had managed to find eventually petered out. Horrified by what appeared to be happening to me, I prayed for rescue and instinctively turned to writing as my one navigational aid.

Contemplation would be my theme; this much was clear. Contemplation had always attracted me. It was a passion with which I'd grown up; the passion for seeing. As a child, for example, I found it the most natural thing in the world to stand at my bedroom window before going to bed, gazing out into the night sky. I didn't think about it; it was nothing extraordinary in my experience. On the contrary, this night-time absorption came naturally to me, as it does to many children. It was my instinctive way of making friends with the darkness, that infinite universe which stretched out beyond the limits of consciousness. I seem to have intuited that the unknown of it all nourished and expanded my heart, that I was somehow intimately related to it and that it was inviting me out into a myriad of mysterious and exciting possibilities.

Nearly all the books I had read about contemplation back in the 1970s when I entered the convent were written by Christian monks. The writers invariably began by saying that contemplation was a natural human experience, a receptive, appreciative response to life, to nature and to beauty. But for them, it was clear that contemplation was also a profession; a religious profession. The few people called to this profession formed part of an ascetic tradition with roots going back to the deserts of Egypt and to the pre-Christian quasi-monastic communities of antiquity.

I knew that the passion for seeing I'd grown up with was something innate. It had been quite instinctive and natural for me to delight in the stars and revel in the vastness of the great unknown. It was in fact an act of faith, pure, simple and gigantic, as only a child is capable of. But as well as being innate, contemplation also felt essential enough to me to be my profession. I felt that it was no less a life profession for me than for the sisters who had taken life vows at the convent. But was it essentially *religious?*

The passion for seeing was rather different from going to church. The minister hadn't spoken about the great unknown at church. He spoke about God and Jesus and the Holy Spirit, who were all in some way related to the great unknown as far as I was concerned, but having been named by the church, they belonged to the daylight world, which was one step removed from the exhilaration and intimacy of night.

Perhaps I knew deep down that, for me at least, contemplation wasn't essentially religious, and that ultimately it wasn't going to be confined to a religious enclosure. To admit this knowing and make the decision to leave the convent was hard though, because it was the only place I'd found where contemplation seemed to be recognized and honoured as a legitimate way of life. What's more, it was the first time I'd found a community of people with whom I felt a deep affinity and a true sense of belonging.

If my kind of contemplation wasn't essentially a religious profession, what *was* it? And where was I to practice it, if not in a convent?

*

It wasn't until I found myself in Amsterdam, almost twenty-five years after leaving the convent, that I had the chance to start exploring contemplation again and to see what the intervening years had taught me about it.

There was just one guideline which became clear to me early in the writing process: I had to let contemplation take the lead. Form and content had to be decided as far as possible by the contemplative process. Contemplation had to be allowed to speak for itself.

At first, the process was exhilarating. There were creative breakthroughs and surprises. Scrolling down through the results of an internet search on contemplation one morning, for example, I came across Thomas Merton sandwiched between a rimmed soup bowl and a lipstick (yes, there *is* a lipstick called Contemplation).

The incongruity shocked me at first; a more bizarre juxtaposition would be hard to imagine. Following the shock, though, came a sense of relief and refreshment, together with a slowly dawning sense that despite all the insights and inspiration I had gleaned from years spent researching the literature of contemplative traditions, despite all the passion and prayerfulness which pervaded them, I had here stumbled upon something which, without my knowing it, I had been missing.

The search engine, unfettered by gifts of discernment and discrimination, had achieved by accident what the rest of us can only hope to receive by grace. What I glimpsed in that moment was a contemplation temporarily released from the cells in which it had been refined and confined. There on my screen, momentarily liberated from its self-consciousness and lofty pretensions, contemplation was set free to fall (flanked by the soup bowl and the lipstick) back down to earth.

Was it my imagination, or did I catch sight of Merton with a glint in his eye, chuckling at the delightful impropriety of it?

This, then, became the vision which inspired me: a contemplation less composed; a contemplation with its feathers ruffled and its disciplines transgressed. A multi-faceted, many-layered contemplation; less a state or practice to be achieved and more a process of deepening intimacy with senses I already had, senses innate, yet dormant in me—in all of us—which told me that the universe was fundamentally trustworthy and that if I let myself go I would bounce back!

As months rolled into years, however, the passion didn't quite pan out as I'd hoped. By now I was in the middle of the menopause, my self-confidence was plummeting and, far from producing a book, the messy, metamorphosing process of writing seemed to be leading only to increasingly frequent and debilitating migraines. I had always been in good health, but now, the more I wrote, the more headaches I seemed to get, and the more the book seemed to be disintegrating. I kept telling myself to stop trying, yet still I seemed compelled to write.

In the end there was nothing else for it but to admit that my old life—my *young* life—was gone forever. The old identity was dissolving and there seemed nothing I could do to stop it.

Among the things which helped sustain me during these years was a new kind of community, which gradually began to assemble itself around me. This community couldn't be defined institutionally or located geographically; rather it seemed to arise haphazardly, often through reading. The men and women who made up this community came from many different cultures and walks of life. Among them were musicians, monks, artists, dancers and poets. Some of them were well known, others less so. Although I didn't know them personally, and although we had no common background, we did, nevertheless, have something in common, and this common element became clear to me one day in the words of Georgia O'Keeffe:

> Whether you succeed or not is irrelevant, there is no such thing. Making your unknown known is the important thing—and keeping the unknown always beyond you . . .
> What is the difference whether I win or lose—I am a very small moment in time.

> Roxana Robinson, *Georgia O'Keeffe*

This new company that had gathered itself around me comprised people who, in one way or another, had embarked on an unknown course. It was a core community of people who *cared* for the unknown and I recognized myself in the wholeheartedness with which they threw themselves into it. I, like them, was sojourning for a while in the realms of the not-yet-integrated in pursuit of deeper awareness.

It wasn't bound by time or space, but I began to sense that this new company was nevertheless being intensely lived. It was a community of deep-divers, up-rooters, wire-cutters, free-fallers and their engagement with the unknown, even if carried out in solitude, was nevertheless an intense kind of activity on behalf of the world because no vision, no truly inspired seeing, is possible without it.

One member of this company was a nineteenth-century Bengali man. Some people questioned his sanity; others considered him a saint. What was clear to me was that *Ramakrishna Paramahamsa* was a simple man with a spectacular passion for God, and his life story and that of his direct disciples was to have a profound effect on me.

Although I had visited India twice by the time I found out about Sri Ramakrishna, I didn't know very much about the Hindu religion, so I was as perplexed as I was stunned by what I learned. In particular, what drew me to him was the depth of his devotion to the goddess Kali.

As the primeval creative power of the universe, Mother Kali is multi-dimensional and spectacularly proliferating. She takes her devotees way beyond the realm of intellect and reason. Together with Her spouse, Shiva, She it is who creates, dissolves and sustains the entire universe.

Kali often appears far removed from the image we associate with a mother goddess. Sometimes portrayed with wild, unbound hair and teeth sharp as fangs, She seems to be a fearsome and intimidating figure, making it hard to conceive how She could ever be approached or experienced as beautiful and compassionate. However, it is precisely the resolution of this apparent paradox which the devotee may come to perceive through worshipping Her.

What Kali offers her devotees is a way of incorporating

uncomfortable, uncontrollable realities. No matter how the disordered, unpredictable aspects of life may manifest, seeing them, accepting them and appropriating them through Her enables the devotee ultimately to be liberated from the fear of them. Kali comes as All: the wished for along with the un-wished for, the convenient along with the inconvenient. Whatever form or aspect She takes at any one moment, the devotee learns to *feel* Her as beautiful, and so enters a deeper, more intimate engagement with whatever life brings. She is death. She is also the death of Death. What Mother Kali dissolves, ultimately, is ignorance.

I was not, and never have been, interested in devotional cults or in the tantric practices sometimes associated with Kali's worship. It was purely through deep appreciation of Sri Ramakrishna's surrender that I also came to appreciate Her loveliness. It was his beholding of Her that inspired my own. I was fascinated by how Kali was seen through the eyes of his devotion and the more I read about him and his followers, the more I was drawn into the heart of his gaze. Reason was unable to grasp any of it. His surrender simply struck me as Kali's magnificence; the two were one, and this One was resplendent. I had never seen anything like it, and the more I looked, the more I seemed to be alight with it.

By now, several more years had passed. I continued to write as and when I could, but despite the encouragement I drew from this new company, I was starting seriously to question whether embarking on this contemplative writing enterprise had been such a good idea.

Truth be told, it was revealing rather more than I had bargained for. Although ordinary, everyday activities such as shopping, ironing and cooking continued on the surface, the reference points I'd always relied on to orient myself in life and establish identity had all but disappeared. Country had gone, job had gone, financial independence had gone, language had gone, and nothing seemed to be arising to take its place.

Then one day a more gentle light began to pervade the process. I saw myself looking at what I was writing much as I would look at a shell or a pearl. There was affection in this seeing, and a deep tenderness. At first this was nothing more than a momentary glimpse, but it lasted long enough for me to recognize that a softer spirit had begun to permeate, and that a wholly different mental atmosphere prevailed here. I had known satisfaction, even excitement, during the writing process, but writing had never before been touched by this warmth and loving-kindness.

What had happened to cause this change was a shift in perception. My perspective had changed. I was now the one witnessing both the writer and the writing, and this one had no personal investments. This one wasn't trying to maintain a precarious hold on any structure; it had no story to compose, no self to secure, no rights to proclaim or wrongs to correct. This one was seeing wholly and this one was free.

The book I had *thought* I was writing arose from habits of mind formed by conditioning. It was the story I had believed in—the story I believed myself to be. Contemplation on the other hand is all-seeing; its only purpose had been to draw me deeper into the heart's more expansive view. Here, nothing needed to be put in order because nothing was out of order. Nothing needed to be put together because nothing was ever apart. Indeed, *I* was not a part. Love had entered the picture and "my story" was at an end.

So, what eventually emerged as the next section of this book, which I call "Picturing", is a record of some scenes from my life as I have reimagined it. They are a hotchpotch of seeming happenings; views of an identity steadily becoming dis-enthralled with itself and having to find a new way of looking.

I have called this record Picturing because it can best be read as a photo album is "read". Each reflection can be seen as a snapshot from the exploration of contemplation. These snapshots are ordered chronologically, but as with a photo album in which dates and place names may be missing or faded, so these "snapshots" capture random moments and isolated incidents. Identifying details may be missing and decades may pass between one picture and the next.

Contemplation is timeless, so liberties had to be taken with time. The present tense may be used even when an event in childhood is described. Also, I didn't always edit out the thoughts and reflections of an adult mind when writing of events which apparently happened in childhood because, from the contemplative perspective, the concepts "child" and "adult" are absent.

Following the Picturing section there is a Review section in which I summarize what this passion for seeing has come to mean for me now; how it emerged through the Picturing process, and how it has transformed my understanding of that calling which took me to the convent several decades ago.

This album of snapshots is a miscellany. Some of the pictures are detailed close-ups, others wide-angle landscapes. Some contain narrative, some are abstract, others impressionistic. Some images may be read quickly, others invite a more lingering gaze. Finally, as with any album, what is made of the pictures depends on what the seer chooses to make of them.

# II

# Picturing

*Write the vision;*
*Make it plain upon the tablets . . .*
*For still the vision awaits its time;*
*it hastens to the end—it will not lie.*
*If it seem slow, wait for it;*
*it will surely come, it will not delay.*

Hab. 2:2–3

Moving down the tunnel of my dream towards the light, I find a lamb just born; its body is still damp and warm to the touch. Easing the lamb gently aside, I squeeze past and emerge into a living room. The lights are on; a clock is ticking.

Standing alone by my bedroom window, four-year-old feet bare on the lino floor, I'm gazing out over the yellow lights and roof-tops of the town, to the stars and the distant darkness of the great unknown beyond.

The door opens behind me and my mother comes in to say goodnight. She sees me standing alone in the evening light. "You're not happy," she says, her voice trembling, her jaw tense. Realizing she's almost in tears, I clamber into bed, horrified. "I am happy," I say, desperate to reassure her. "*Really* I am." She tucks me up, kisses me and leaves the room.

Overwhelmed with embarrassment to have been caught doing something apparently so frightful, I lie still in the shocked silence, trying to fall asleep.

The rocking-boat stands alongside the swings, the slide and the roundabout in the park behind our house. It isn't a real boat of course; we simply imagine it's a boat and that we, with our cheeks flushed and the wind in our hair, are all sailors, bound for far-off lands.

One day, rocking in the boat as usual, I happen to look up above the tops of the trees at the end of the park into the clouds and blue sky beyond and as I look, the laughter and children's chatter around me subsides and I am suddenly alone in the emptiness of sky, filled with an enormous knowing: when you're dead, you're dead for ever . . . and ever . . . and ever . . . and ever . . .

*Ever-and-everness* rises and falls with the rhythmic rocking of the boat until I am filled with it. *Ever-and-everness* is simple and vast; comforting and constant as breathing, as life itself. *Ever-and-everness* can hold my weight like the sea, and play will go on.

New smells have been seeping out from under the door of the front room.

I know the smell of turpentine. This is what my father uses when he's painting the walls and window frames. But my father isn't decorating now. If he was, the doors and windows would be open and I'd know about it.

What's happening in the front room is secret. We used to keep my pram in the front room, but I haven't seen that for a long time now. Mostly the front room is kept tidy and ready for special occasions when visitors come and biscuits get put out on the blue plate my parents got as a wedding present. Now, though, something else is happening in that room—with turpentine.

Today, when the house is quiet, I open the door just a crack and peer in. Something is propped up on the table against a pile of books and covered with a cloth. There are brushes in a jar and tubes of paint lying around. I've never seen anything like this before, but I know it must be my mother's painting. I've never seen her paint before. I've only ever known her to make cakes. But this must be what it is. She must do it in the evening when I'm in bed.

Quietly I go further into the room, reach out a hand and lift the cloth.

What I see before me is a swirling blue sea and two sea-creatures rising up out of the depths. They are arching monstrously, locked into one another like the wrestlers I've seen on television. Far below, under the arch formed by the twisted bulk of the monster wrestlers, walks a small girl with long dark hair. She is wearing a pink dress. I know immediately that she is me. I also know I shouldn't be looking, and that this can't be talked about.

I replace the cloth and silently leave the room.

The painting disappeared, just like the pram. I never saw it again.

"What is it you *want*?"
I am out shopping with my mother; we are standing outside Williams Bros. the butchers. I know at once that this is not an ordinary kind of question, because I can feel my mother's embarrassment. She has tried to make it sound more casual by dropping

it into the context of decisions about whether to have lamb chops or mince for tea. But I know immediately she isn't referring to the meat.

Surprised as I am by the question and the awkwardness surrounding it, an image comes to mind immediately. The image is of a large room with French windows at one end. The windows are open, there are white curtains blowing gently in the breeze and sunlight is streaming into the room. The image reminds me of the studio I go to twice a week for my dance classes; it's a spacious room, filled with music and movement and bright summer air.

"Space . . ." I say, "definitely more space."

My mother decides on the mince. Nothing more is said about the space.

Sitting in the school library, flicking through pages of career books, I gaze hopefully at pictures of nurses and air hostesses. The more the decision about what I'm going to *do* with my life looms, the more fraught it seems to become and the more tightly the possibilities close in around me.

So when we're asked at church if we want to be confirmed, I see it in the context of life choices and career decisions. My mother makes me a white dress for the occasion, and when the bishop's hands come to rest briefly on my head, I am absolutely clear that, for better or worse, I am dedicating my life to God. I am sixteen.

The little silver-and-blue medallion containing the image of St Thérèse isn't jewellery. I don't wear it. That would be too Catholic. I keep it in a box under my bed, together with the photos of Rex Harrison and Audrey Hepburn that I had cut out of the programme after we'd been up to London to see *My Fair Lady*.

I bought the medallion in the basilica gift shop during our trip to Normandy last year. I had no idea someone could do with their life what Thérèse had done with hers. I was desperate to know more about her, but the booklet I bought was in French. I stared at the words for hours, willing them to make sense, but my French wasn't up to it. Still, I gleaned what I could and knew for sure that this was something I'd been looking for all my life but until now hadn't known existed.

Once back in Britain though, the memory of Thérèse faded. She was simply not compatible with the Church of England or the suburbs of North London where I live.

I like our church. I love the way the sun shines through the stained glass windows, sending blue and violet splashes across the pages of my hymn book. I like the starkness and silence of Good Friday and the shock of the empty tomb at Easter. I like the stories of ordinary people who dream dreams and see visions; before whom seas part, and rocks roll away, and I like the strange prophets who live in the desert on locusts and wild honey. The winds of the Spirit blow through me too. Bells ring. Tongues of flame leap and dance. Mountains and valleys clap their hands. It's a huge and magnificent panorama, this whole company of heaven inside the doors of one small church. My universe expands here and my spirit breathes.

But worship in our church is performed with as little emotion as possible. Going to church is a good thing, but once a week is enough. Attending church twice on a Sunday is verging on the excessive. Two candles on the altar are acceptable, but incense certainly isn't.

Our town simply is not big enough for a basilica and the Church of England, as far as I know, doesn't have monks or nuns, and isn't all that comfortable with saints either. Our church is a reasonable and restrained church and seems a long way from being able to tolerate (much less appreciate) the heat and passion generated by one such as Thérèse in the extravagant presumption of her desire for union with God.

Sometimes, before going to sleep, I take the medallion out of its box and look at Thérèse. Not being Catholic, I know I have no right to her really so I keep her hidden. I would never speak to anyone about her and I know, though no one has actually told me, that her way is "foreign" and that she has been banished.

I'm sure that I've given my life to God, but still the question remains: what am I going to *be*? What do I have to become? My church simply doesn't seem to offer any career possibilities. There is, of course, the minister. He's a religious professional, but he's also a man and a lot less inspiring than St Thérèse. Anyway, his is not the kind of job I'm looking for.

What then *am* I looking for?

I had hoped I might become a dance teacher, but it rather looks as though I'll be going to secretarial college. I'm not sure that I've chosen to become a secretary; still less am I sure that being a secretary is God's will for me. But I leave school with qualifications in shorthand and typing and very little else. I'm told it's always something to fall back on.

This is the track I've been on all along, apparently. My mother was a secretary, so I needn't have worried. The teachers seem pleased; perhaps I am too. I allow myself to be convinced because it's 1968, revolutions are breaking out and anything is possible. Girls in my class are running away from home, getting into flower-power, going to rock concerts at the weekend, and experimenting with sex—or saying they are. Meanwhile Thérèse of Lisieux lies under my bed with her roses; promising, illicit, beating out secrets.

I stick a poster of the Golden Gate Bridge on my wardrobe door. Somehow God's plan will be revealed. A dream will be realized. My life will evolve into a grand passion and I too will scatter roses down from heaven.


"How do you pray?" Sister Madelene, the Guest Mistress, is walking with me through the fields to the guest house. Her question takes me aback. Nothing has ever prepared me to answer such a question, but obviously she expects an answer. I am horrified.

Ever since I discovered that such things as Anglican convents existed, I've been coming here once or twice a year for private retreats, but I hadn't expected this.

It's not an unreasonable question, of course. I know I should have an answer, and I know the answer should involve Jesus. Jesus is supposed to be central, but the fact is he has never figured very prominently on the horizon of my prayer life. Prayer is the great unknown: the sky, the stars, the empty tomb. But that's not the answer.

Prayer has always just been present. I've never thought about it and I certainly didn't know it was possible to *talk* about it. Even if I could talk about it, I fear my answer would be wrong and it would become obvious that I'm a fraud and the sisters would refuse to allow me to come here anymore.

It's such a relief to have found the company of these women, who don't find this life strange; who aren't embarrassed by it, or fearful of it. To give the wrong answer now would be to risk losing this precious refuge.

So I let the moment pass in silence. But I continue to think about the question.

For me, prayer is simply mixed in with life. It clings and swirls like mist among the pine trees on the hills opposite the convent. It piles up like the plums in my basket, ripe and round. The fact is I've never really noticed prayer before, just as I've never really noticed plums. Prayer has been around all my life, like gratitude. Prayer is what arises when life is as nourishing as this.

Prayer is the space I'm longing for, and the relief of not being thought odd for wanting it. Prayer is what happens when I notice a gap in the universe and dive in.

But none of this is an answer to the question of *how.*

The question of *method* had simply never occurred to me.

It isn't until the Mother Superior meets me and takes me towards the door which leads from the visitors' sitting-room to the nuns' quarters that the step I'm taking becomes crystal clear to me. I'm no longer staying temporarily as a guest. For the first time, I'm now moving into the enclosure where my new life will begin. My friend and flat-mate, who has brought me here, will be leaving tomorrow to drive back to London and get on with her life without me.

In my bedroom I find a single bed, a chest of drawers, a small table, and a wash stand with jug and bowl. On my bed lie two towels and two freshly laundered and pressed white veils. Two coat hangers hang on a hook on the back of the door. The walls are plain white. On the table is a small blue vase of yellow chrysanthemums and a card signed by all the sisters, wishing me well at the start of this six-month postulancy. The sincerity of their welcome warms me as I unpack my bible, my sewing basket, apron, underwear and overalls. I'm allotted a place at the back of the chapel next to the other postulant. After Evensong, supper and Compline, I prepare for bed, listening to the autumn wind as it whistles through the cracks around the window pane, wondering what lies before me.

Silence is to be observed all day apart from exchanging absolutely essential, work-related information or instructions. Silence doesn't just refer to talking; it is meant to refer to all extraneous "noise". The rules about talking are relaxed during recreation each evening and on Sunday afternoons, when short walks around the grounds, or meetings with guests, are allowed.

Despite the silence, or perhaps because of it, I quickly become aware that there are some strong personalities here. No one is trying to be noticed; it's simply clear that these are determined women, all with their own characters and quirks. One or two of them really sparkle and radiate a lightness of spirit that is as infectious as it is refreshing.

Although everyone is wearing the same habit and looks outwardly uniform, it becomes possible to identify people by the smallest gestures and movements. A nun can be recognized by her walk or posture, by the way a hymn book is held, or by the way a raincoat is hung on a hook. Without the distraction of talking, these small gestures become noticeable, and I appreciate them deeply as part of the gift and the fabric of our common life.

One Sunday afternoon, soon after my arrival, Sister Elizabeth, one of the older nuns, invites me to go for a walk with her. Taking what we think to be a shortcut back to the convent, we find the paths increasingly overgrown, until eventually our way is all but blocked by waist-high bracken, stinging nettles and fallen branches. As we bash away with sticks to flatten the briars, which are scratching our ankles and legs, Sister Elizabeth turns to me, laughing. "This is tough-going . . . actually, it's a very good metaphor for the religious life!"

The dairy is the place where I begin my working day. It's here that I wait before sunrise for the nun in charge of milking the Jersey cows to bring the warm milk up from the cow shed. First, the cream has to be separated from the milk. If I concentrate hard and hold my breath in order to steady the hand holding the metal "skimmer", the cream comes off smoothly like folds of pale yellow velvet. Then, once the cream is separated, I set it aside to be made into butter later by another sister. Then the milk has to be bottled and all the equipment sterilized with scalding hot water, which turns the dairy into a sauna. Then I hang up my apron, and begin looking forward to breakfast and, *finally*, a cup of coffee!

Another of my jobs is to pick up the plums that have blown down during the night. I am stunned by the colours of them as they pile up in my basket. There are crimson and magenta plums, burgundy and cobalt-blue plums; some about to burst their skins, others already seeping juice. All of them have a silver sheen and they are sparkling with dew.

Here at the convent I begin to sense something of the kind of wholeness and spaciousness I've been looking for all my life. It's a wholeness which comes not only from the way the life is proportioned but also from the way it is concentrated. It's as if the daily round of work, worship and prayer gather life into one single-pointed desire. Be it driving tractors, digging potatoes, harvesting hay, operating printing presses, cooking for guests or milking cows, the different daily activities are only important insofar as they re-collect attention. Regardless of whatever *jobs* the sisters are doing, recollection is what they are absorbed in. And it is this, the wholeness of life here, which draws me in.

It isn't purely, or even particularly, focused in chapel. The wholeness is like a sudden intensification of awareness which can flood over me at any time. It most often arises in the context of ordinary daily activities. It might come for example out in the fields on sunny mornings while I'm hanging out the laundry breathing the fragrance of resin from the pines on the hills opposite. Or when the wind sends the bright sheets snapping and flapping against my face. In such moments, all the elements of life seem to meet and merge and I can almost taste the zest of them.

Perhaps, where faith is concerned, I have to start again from scratch.

This is the thought which comes to me while I am out walking in the Dales today, and the more I reflect on it, the more organic and elemental faith begins to feel, and the more I seem to catch the scent of something which engages my heart and fills me with fresh hope.

The only place to start now is with the bare bones of my own experience; with the trees, the grassland, the clouds and the soft rain. Start with the raw materials of life surrounding me out on these moors. Start with the elements and the seasons, the silvery tracks of snails and the seagulls swooping; the scent of peat and heather, and the sharp, crisp wind.

I think about them as I walk: the bare bones of this moorland faith. It may turn out to be only a simple faith, but it does at least feel reliable because it's rooted in my being and grows through my daily living and knowing.

It's not so much a turning away from church or religion, more a *distilling*, bringing faith down to earth from the elaboration of creeds and doctrines to the essentials, to the faith I cannot *be* without.

There's an enormous relief in letting the weight of the church fall from my shoulders.

It may take courage to have this kind of faith, to come into closer alignment with nature's purposes and to move from the familiar faith of a church to a faith born from the heart of matter. But I'm out again in the elements, where I belong, and I sense it as a great adventure.

My fore-mothers left school at the age of eleven (if they went to school at all) and got jobs as servants in the big houses at the other end of town. They lived in attics and got up at four o'clock in the morning to lay fires and clean other people's shoes. If they were lucky they got one day off a month to go home and visit their families. On Sundays, my great-aunt told me, she and all the other household staff piled into a horse-drawn carriage and followed their employer's carriage to church, where they sat in special servants' pews at the back.

My fore-mothers spent their young lives in service. Their place was clear. I know it too, the comfortable anonymity of this place at the back. But is it mine, this line of women who knew their place? I want to stay here with my fore-mothers; I want them to want me to stay. To leave is to desert them, to *be* deserted, whereas staying in line feels safe. So, all I have to do is let the safety of this place lay claim to me. All I have to do is let my eyelids grow heavy with the weight of wanting to stay, and let my limbs sink into the slow pulse of this sleep forever.

But just as I'm starting to doze off I catch a glimpse of my fore-mothers. They are standing now, smiling and waving me off . . . Their arms are raised as if in blessing.

Then, out of nowhere, a thought occurs; an impossible, almost unthinkable thought:

*What if I'm the one who has to step out of line?*
*What if I'm the one who has to step outside;*
*where there is nowhere to step?*

The poster I saw in the window of the Quaker Meeting House recently read: "I pin my hopes to quiet processes and small circles, in which vital and transforming events take place." I've decided to go to Meeting next Sunday.

The main figure in the dream is an Egyptian woman. She doesn't have the traditionally painted Egyptian eyes but an expert verifies that the face is Egyptian.

Someone tells me that on her death in ancient Egypt, provision was made for her to be brought back to life sometime in the future, which is the reason why she had not been mummified. She has communicated through a séance and given instructions regarding the materials and processes necessary to bring her back to life.

It appears that the Egyptian woman can be controlled. The group of people I'm with can be bring her to life and we can also put her to "sleep" again. At first I like this woman, but after some time, we start to realize that she is in fact evil, sent by the devil to create havoc among us. I'm now also aware of the presence of her opposite—a woman in a light or white gown, but this woman hardly makes any impression on me at all.

When we realize what chaos and destruction the Egyptian woman is causing among us, we know that we'll have to try to stop her rising, but by this time she has established herself, she can now control her own rising and we have virtually lost control of her.

I can see the coffin from which she rises. It's small, made of clay, covered in hieroglyphics on the top and sides, and on the bottom are two rows of hieroglyphics running the length of the coffin. These two rows are especially interesting because they seem like tracks on the base of the coffin and one of the symbols is in the shape of a horse. The only way I can think of to stop her rising is to encase the coffin in lead, but someone suggests that to cover it with marble would be more effective.

I don't know whether we were successful in stopping her.

Another séance last night. A group of women, including some witches, are telling me in the dream to meet them tomorrow at midnight. A scream rises from somewhere within me. It doesn't come from my mouth but I know in the dream that it's me scream-ing. The scream echoes through my body and I wake, terrified of this message from the beyond. Who are these women who want to meet me?

Then I go back to sleep and dream again. This time I'm on board a ship in a rough sea being thrown against the rigging. I see a man in Gestapo uniform on the other side of the ship and I know that this is the surprise attack I'd been told to expect. I have a choice now: abandon ship or defend it. I know my job is to defend it, so I swing out on a rope knowing that the return swing will give me extra force. The man doesn't see me coming so I have the advantage of surprise and I kick him using all the momentum of the return swing. When he sees me he calls out to his friend: "Enemy Wasp!" and he shoots at me with an artificial gun. I'm annoyed that he has shot first. I shoot back, but it's his victory. I hadn't known that weap-ons were allowed.

Back now on my own side of the ship, I see a letter that has been written to me; it has also been written *by* me. "My darling," it begins, "we are only just alive."

The dreams I've been having lately are disturbing. They leave me with a strong impression that all is not well and that I need to get help.

Searching for a book in the university library catalogue this morning, I notice something that looks like a black stain on the page. It's only when I try to brush it off that I realize it isn't on the page but in my sight.

Then I look around me and notice that this mark is all over the place. It's as though there's a small patch blocking out part of the vision in my right eye.

As I leave the library a headache begins and by the time I get back to my room half of my head is throbbing and I'm starting to feel sick—and scared. I call the doctor and go to bed.

The doctor arrives, examines me and diagnoses migraine. I've never experienced anything like this before but I'm relieved at least to know what it is. The doctor thinks it's probably caused by too much studying or stress before my final exams. She thinks it will go away.

The eyes are unmoving, the gaze attentive. She looks out at me, with her pale skin and oval face, as if through a window, from her day into mine.

The face is turned expectantly towards me, as if waiting for an answer to a question asked just seconds ago: *How do you respond?*

I came across this reproduction last week in an art shop down a little alley-way close to the Quaker Meeting House. I was so struck by the steadiness of attention portrayed here that I immediately bought the card, framed it and put it on my desk.

This isn't the flat, abstract, impersonal regard of the Byzantine icon. It's not that other-worldly face. This face is wholly human and personally present.

I know there's significance in this face, but the more I reflect on it and wonder about it, the more it seems to resist any attempts to make meaning of it. Or maybe it's just a kind of meaning which won't be grasped.

The only thing I seem able to *do* in relation to this woman and her quiet question is receive impressions; notice and enjoy her as one might notice and enjoy patterns the wind makes as it blows through sand.

Whatever it is I have to see just has to be allowed to germinate, leaving me with no option but to turn my attention back to the daily tasks, the commitments and appointments, which are easier to fix and which seem to be leading somewhere.

Six o'clock in the morning and I'm preparing breakfast in the retreat centre where I work, arranging cereals on the counter, slicing bread on the meat-slicer, unfreezing orange juice under the hot tap because someone forgot to take it out of the freezer to thaw last night . . . when quite unexpectedly, my attention is drawn outside. It's as though my name is being called, but there's no sound, no name, just an inexplicable sense of longing to *see,* and of being led outside.

So I step outside into the garden and look. But where to look when the whole world beckons; when nature points everywhere and nowhere all at once? How to respond, when looking in any one direction necessitates turning my back on another; when every attraction becomes, simultaneously, a distraction?

Standing in the fresh, cool air of this early morning bewilderment, I watch the first rays of sun creep quietly over the branches of the hemlock tree. Nothing more seems demanded, nothing but my presence, my attention and my capacity to enjoy.

Yet I'm also aware of a vague sense of puzzlement and frustration. Complete as this moment is, I know that it's possible to see more, *much* more. Somehow I know that there are eyes all over, and that 360-degree seeing is possible.

After a few moments I reluctantly return to the kitchen to finish my work, but the sense of being called, and the longing to see more widely and deeply lingers all morning.

For so long we have struggled not to be gods
and this constant denial of our divinity
has so sapped our strength
so shrivelled our minds
that we are almost content
almost convinced
of our not-godness
The truth is that we are all gods
born with the burning sun in our grasp


Three years I've been away in America, but now, like a cicada emerging from its long underground gestation, it's time for me to shake the damp earth from my ears, unwrap my wings, climb high into the bright, singing branches and fly home.

The landscape recedes as I take off: fields of corn, sweeping plains, wide desert reaches . . . all wash back into what will shortly become memory. I will miss the fire-flies and the song of the cicada on summer evenings. I will miss the red-winged black-bird and the crimson flash of the cardinal in the late winter snow. I will miss the chipmunk, the possum, the humming-bird . . . the whole company now disbanding.

Far below I see the Statue of Liberty looking lost among the sky-scrapers, shrouded in the blue-grey haze of a sticky New York evening. To me, she seems to symbolize the Benedictine vow of stability; the vow to stay put in one place. She is balanced, dispassionate; firm in her liberty, while the rest of us fly by, in search of ours.

In a few moments the whole set will be struck, the lights will gradually dim, the flight attendants will come round with drinks and hot towels, and on the other side of the Atlantic I will wake . . . to what? My home? I fear I shall not know myself in my own country.

The grief in my chest suddenly rises like an army to do battle in my throat and I fight to subdue it. It's my choice after all, to go home.

All too soon, before I'm ready for it, the world comes rushing up again to peer and poke and find out what has become of me. My suitcase wheels squeak as I trundle through Heathrow Arrivals. Everyone seems to be staring at me. A man stops to help me with my cases at Kings Cross station and tears of exhaustion and gratitude spill over as I thank him.

Tightly packed terraced houses fly past the train window. The land seems to have shrunk. The countryside is lush and green. Black-and-white cows obligingly dot the hillsides. Fishermen meditate under bright umbrellas and canal boats float peacefully end to end. It's all so familiar, so picturesque.

I try to strike up a conversation with a woman while waiting at the bus-stop. She eyes me suspiciously. I've forgotten how to be British and I'm wearing the wrong kind of clothes. I am out of place; out of space. How to find myself now?

And what of liberty? Have I left her behind?

I remember the moment in America when I was most homesick. It was, strangely, when I heard French being spoken. It reminded me of childhood holidays with my parents in France. I longed to come back then, but not to England or to Britain. I longed to be surrounded again by foreign languages and pavement cafés and buildings with roots which go down for miles and dark, musty interiors with flagstone floors and the smell of damp disintegrating walls. I loved the brilliance of America, the sun, the deep blue autumnal skies and the optimism. But my spirit longed for a softer light, for mist and cloud.

Seen from America, home became Europe. America has made me European. It's the way I see now. And now that I'm back I want to know what's happening to us all in Europe. I shall soon be moving to Brussels.

A re you out there? Will you write? These are the first thoughts which greet me as I wake these days. Each morning I hope to hear from you. Have you got my letter?

Infuriating silence.

I know that the intensity of our gaze will change over time. I know that the days will now pass relentlessly through our lives like water, clarifying but also inevitably diluting. Our letters crossing the Atlantic will be written with loyalty, with love, but with diminishing desire.

This knowledge fills me with regret and the disappointment of betrayal. Must it always be so? Does every momentous passion fade into the shadows of an uneasy forgetfulness?

I am shocked at my indiscretion, shamed by the apparent ease with which I can grieve the loss of one love, even as I wait expectantly for that which will next present itself to compete for my heart's affection. I am weary of such inconstancy; weary of what seems to be my inability to believe in the uniqueness of one passion, to grasp it and live it with faithfulness.

S hall we ever grow into the story of that perfect friendship you dream of? I dreamed it once too, but it seems that I lost that dream many life times ago. I was not indiscriminate or casual in my loving; perhaps I was searching so hard I simply forgot what I was looking for, or perhaps I have never really known.

Love is a word I want to be able to mean. But sometimes it's as though there is a panel of judges listening in as I say it, awarding points for technical merit, artistic interpretation, sincerity and style. Before I know it, the judges disagree, and love slips out blurred and smudged, as if half my mouth were numb. And I fear it shows.

I want to be able to say it and mean it, but I fear I've spoken it too often without knowing it, and that now it may be too late.

Perhaps that's why the Hebrews made YHWH unpronounceable. Better to be silenced before the silence of the great incomprehensible. At least then there's no mistaking it. No danger then of the Infinite getting blurred, or slipping out smudged.

*Life moves on, passion fades, people change, move on . . . Nothing lasts forever, you have to be philosophical, reasonable . . .*

Whose lines are these? Whose voice is it? I don't remember anyone ever actually saying these lines, yet I've just caught them running through my mind, like a script, and I realize only now that I seem to have heard them forever.

Perhaps I'm usually reassured by this adult, philosophical voice. It makes sense, and I like to make sense. Life dies. Love burns. It seems to ring true. But today these once reassuring words make me unutterably tired. They are heavy, joyless, faithless words, and I no longer have the heart for them.

I was on a plane once where all the wires got crossed. The trick was to try to find the person on the other side of the plane whose switch operated your reading light.

All the passengers were calling out to one another: "Your switch works my light . . ." "OK, who's got your switch then?" "Try that one over there . . ."

It was like a game in the end. It didn't do much for our confidence in the workings of the plane but it was great for passing the time.

I see now what has happened. Certain wires have got crossed. Love is switched on and along comes loss—or the fear of it—like a foregone conclusion.

Some part of me seems, secretly, to be expecting loss; some part of me has decided that loss is inevitable and that safety resides in the shell-like detached home I carry around on my back.

For fear of being alone I have forced myself to *be* alone, needing to know I can live with the worst of it.

This won't do, of course.

*I've never thought of myself as having a great gift . . . I don't think I have a great gift. It isn't just talent. . . You have to have something else. You have to have a kind of nerve. It's mostly a lot of nerve and a lot of very, very hard work . . . I'm frightened all the time, scared to death. But I never let it stop me. Never.*

Roxana Robinson, *Georgia O'Keeffe*

Perfume from the wisteria lingers in the air as I step out of the glare of the sun into the coolness and shade of the chapel. The silence here is like water, and I'm thirsting for it after the clatter and heat of the day's journey.

I'm spending a few days this Easter on retreat at a convent in southern France. The buildings here are simple; yellow-ochre, rose and rust-coloured. The earth smells of lilac and straw. The red and purple flesh of the orange I ate for lunch reminded me how parched I am. Gold-winged butterflies accompany me on my walk up the mountain and I find some tiny wild orchids, their pale purple petals all but hidden in the shadows beneath dark green foliage.

The intensity of colour and light after the greyness of Brussels streets is almost painful to my eyes, but it is a sweet pain, like the pain of blood flowing back into a limb which has long been numb.

A deeply tanned man with long grey hair and intense eyes of the same colour walks past me, eating a dandelion.

Four o'clock on Easter Sunday morning. The sky is black as we stand by the bonfire. Stars shine through the branches of the trees around us, flames crackle and spark, warming my face. Then, slowly and stiffly we begin our procession up the silent, sleeping mountain. The long fingers of cypress trees point toward a pale yellow dawn in the eastern sky; only bird song and the snap of twigs underfoot break the silence.

Later in the day communion happens in a room stuffed full of people. Visitors and villagers crowd round tables dressed with brilliant white table cloths, garlands of ivy, bunches of snowdrops, and eggs painted pink, purple and green. There are bowls of curly lettuce leaves, shiny black olives and red radishes cut like water lilies. Wine arrives in big earthenware jars and the bread is brought in, held high in a huge basket, to be broken, blessed and passed from hand to hand: "à toi la gloire; à toi la gloire . . ."

Bodies are all packed in on benches and chairs. There is laughing and talking. Surely this is how it was? Women with no teeth and bad breath telling stories and playing fiddles, men telling jokes, babies being sick, girls in straw hats, youths getting quietly drunk . . . Did the women have a last supper, out there in the kitchen?

Someone knocks over a vase of tulips. There are folk songs now and steaming mugs of coffee, strong and black . . .

*A toi la gloire . . .*

The outdoor chapel has no roof or walls; there are simply log benches to sit on and avenues of cypress trees. The man with long grey hair and bright grey eyes is sitting on a bench not far from me. We are alone. I watch the tiny feet of a gecko basking on the trunk of a tree close to my shoulder and I am longing to stroke its spine.

I think of my friends far away in America, the friends I've so recently left behind. I bring them to life here, in this place of life, and I fold them in the warmth of this moment.

The sun is setting quickly now over the Rhône and the fortifications on the opposite bank are shining rose-pink and gold in the evening light.

Today is the last day of my retreat and I'm looking forward to returning to my life in Brussels; the life I left only four days ago.

Someone is playing a flute in the distance and a warm breeze blows over me as I sit in the town square watching children riding on a merry-go-round.

Before going to catch the night train, I stop at a small restaurant for a meal of chicken with garlic peas, red wine and coffee. Recharged, I make my way to the station, hoping my rucksack will still be in the locker where I left it this morning.

Having rescued my rucksack, I climb on board the train and find my seat. The young woman sitting opposite me is wearing green boots, purple flowered trousers and a blue shirt. She is writing in her journal with a pink pen. I welcome her silently and I enjoy the sight of her enormously. We are both writing. She could be thinking (as I am thinking) that the world could be full of writing women, who are watching other women write. The vision of her, with her flowered trousers and pink pen, is whole. She writes with a mind of her own.

I am in love with my life.

Perhaps
there is only
this everyday
waiting presence of things
and
perhaps
i am giving myself
to a blade of grass
to bread
to thunder
to stone
and
perhaps
in the end
i am warm air
and earth
smelling of honey
and
violets

Last weekend I came across more of the portraits—the originals this time. I literally stumbled over them actually, because they were displayed in a rather dusty glass case on the floor of the Egyptology section of the British Museum. I recognized them immediately as cousins of the reproduction I bought some years ago at the art shop in St. Andrews.

That face has stayed with me as I've travelled around over the years, and now I've been able to find out more about the portraits. They are mummy portraits, dating from the late first century BCE, and most of them were discovered in an area of Egypt known as the Fayoum.

It's not difficult to account for my fascination, of course. The fact that such vulnerable artefacts could have survived and been brought back to the light of day almost two thousand years after they were buried and literally left for dead is reason enough for amazement. Their links with Egyptian mystery religions and death cults makes a potent mixture, guaranteed to stir imagination.

But there's something else: the way they seem to have popped up in my life from time to time in a series of chance encounters. It's almost as if they have been trying to attract my attention; as if they've been determined not to go away until they've been fully seen. Yet what *is* it exactly that has to be seen?

It's not the face of death. True, the face *is* still and composed, but it speaks quite clearly of life; there's speed, intensity and freedom of movement in the brush strokes. True, the portraits were placed squarely in the face of death, but the artists who painted them were known as *zographos*, meaning "those who paint life".

Before these portraits were placed into the casing containing the mummified body, some of them may, apparently, have hung as portraits in the home during the lifetime of the person.

I imagine it hanging there on the wall, something like a solar panel, collecting the warmth, laughter, noise and chatter of family life, the better to help power the soul's journey eventually from the grave, across the waters, into the next sphere.

Living alone is my writing space. My writing space and my living space are sacred. This sacred space is where I live my hallowing; my Sabbath time. It has different textures and colours, this hallowing, and I am learning to move through them all with more or less grace. Sometimes, surprised, I mutter and stumble and think the end is coming. But this is what it means to be hallowed, spirit-shaped, formed by my heart's desire. I wake early and write, casting myself out to sea on my big bed with pillows, happily gazing at clouds.

Sometimes I seem to be surrounded by gentle visitors and loyal guardians. And sometimes it seems as if something huge, pulsating and intoxicating is unfolding.

Yesterday, there was an opening, as if the clouds had parted, and I saw out beyond fear to the place where everything is known and clear.

And a voice somewhere inside me said: *You know now that you have embarked on a journey with no maps and no clothes and each time you look the scenery will change as it speeds past your window. Before you can speak it has changed and you don't know if you are going for a million years or just a day.*

*When was it begun?* I asked.

*When you thought you had lost me; when you walked in the fields and stared at the trees and knew you had to begin again with only the fields and the trees. When you knew you were naked; when you had to stand next to death and look life in the face. That's when it begins.*

And I said: *Yes, I will join you, though I know we are passing beyond all bounds; beyond all bonds tied on earth for safe-keeping.*

There's a miner talking about his work on the radio. He's showing a group of children around the mine. He switches the lights off to show them how dark it can get. The children gasp.

He knows about working in darkness. "Down the mine you listen to the talking beams and you make friends with the rats."

The children giggle uncertainly.

"The beams creak to tell you when the weight above is getting too much to bear, and the rats . . . they know things we can't know. When you don't hear them squeaking anymore, it means they've left, and they don't leave without a reason. It means something's going to happen, so you'd better get out of there, fast."

"If you're lost in a mine you don't light a candle to see your way out. The flame would blow you up. You find the source of air with your nose and follow it."

Taking this miner's wisdom to accompany me, I sit quietly, listening for rats.


Back in Brussels, the first day of teaching is, thankfully, over. It was a delight to come back to my flat this evening, to feel the silence of the place wrap itself around me. I wander around doing exactly what I like: watering plants, opening windows, lighting candles. It is a ritual. So many times this past year I've been so pleased just to be here, just to return to this solitude.

Yesterday I asked a class of teenagers what they thought would happen in the future. "Nuclear war," they said, smiling.

Slept fitfully last night, dreaming of darkening skies and mushroom clouds; waiting for the inevitable. Hoping it would kill me and not leave me half alive. Knowing I must protect my eyes from the flash.

Do I imagine then that protecting my sight will save me?

It is watery weather this morning, with mist fine and gentle enough for mulling and musing. It's one of those days when wood pigeons sink into their feathers and coo comfortably down echoing chimneys; where I step straight into a shroud of evening grey and stay there wrapped in smoky scents, listening to leaves turn purple as plums; listening to trees drop juice.

I would like a relationship which is solid and challenging and spacious. I want to spend long hours gathering the warmth of a well-loved friend. I want the kind of shared history which builds trust; the kind of intimacy which lengthens days and frames my solitude. And I want a cat to step gently round us, licking the maze of fingers intertwined, nudging us persistently to the edge of our lives.

This is my birthday wish as I blow out my candles, sending the light to all the crones in the world. It's the deepest wish I can imagine. I am thirty-nine.


I know that I prefer my lovers and intimate friends in other countries. In this way I put them out of reach so that I don't have to live with the constant fear of losing them, yet at the same time I effectively ensure that I live in a state of loss.

It's becoming intolerable, this self-imposed exile. Is this the way I want to live?

*Listen, in the quiet beauty of your heart.*

*Listen.*

There's a barely perceptible knowledge that another way is possible.

This is all.

There's some new kind of power which at the moment I know nothing of except that it wants to be known and wants to be lived by me. It's a power that acts with me and for me, not in spite of or against me; a power which would never harm me.

All I know is that this power has no comprehension of possession, or of loss, and that if it came to life in me there would be a revolution.

*I was alive that moment when I stood looking at the primroses and the red embers under the hedge. It's a feeling inside you, a kind of peaceful feeling, and yet it's like a flame . . . Why don't people . . . just walk round looking at things? . . . It's the only thing worth having and we don't want it . . . I know it's a good feeling to have. What's more, so does everybody . . . Call it peace, if you like. But when I say peace I don't mean absence of war, I mean peace, a feeling in your guts.*

George Orwell, *Coming up for Air*

Sitting reading in a café today before going to teach my afternoon class, I come upon a phrase which takes hold of me and seems to shake me awake: "this vast inner emptiness is nothing less than the dwelling place of God".

I'm stunned by this phrase. Meaning starts to break in, an immense possibility draws close.

And I'm still thinking about it this evening. I can't quite grasp it but I know I've been touched by these words. It's as though a wasteland is reshaping, hard edges softening, cracks filling in . . .

Something folds round me like a blanket; there is moss to rest in, warmth that I can lean into.

All the creatures of the forest draw close with wide eyes, ready to attend. And I have the feeling that I need never fear loss again.

Finding myself between teaching jobs I register for temporary work with a secretarial agency (the qualifications did, indeed, come in useful). After interviewing me, the woman at the agency sends me to work for the director of a headhunting company. After a few days in the job, it's becoming clear that he wants me to stay.

"Are you looking for a permanent job?" he asks when I go into his office this morning. "Or are you a professional temporary?"

"Professional temporary" is an imaginative possibility so huge it almost makes me gasp. I stare at him in stunned silence for a moment.

I know of course that he's asking about my availability, my readiness to take on a permanent job. But the question registers on an altogether different level. It's the sort of question a Zen master might ask; a question which flies like an arrow, straight to the centre to shock you awake.

Suddenly I'm seeing again with the eyes of a child, standing out in the open, before a wide and exhilarating expanse of sky.

He is still looking at me, waiting for a reply.

"Yes . . ." I say, nodding slowly, "I'm a professional temporary."

It was as if I'd been asked: *Do you want to live your life closed off in a gated community, dimmed and diminished by your own unquestioned assumptions of a preference for permanence? Or do you want to be who you are?*

Until I was asked the question, I hadn't seen that I had a choice. Having seen the choice, the answer was blindingly obvious.

The portraits have been remembered! Public interest in them has grown. They've been brought out of dark museum store-rooms, lifted from floors, retrieved from corners, dusted off, cleaned up and reassembled to form spectacular collections which are travelling the globe, gathering an enthusiastic following.

So now I find myself standing before them once more in the British Museum, this time in the company of hundreds of other admirers, my delight in them shared. And I watch our faces, super-imposed on the ancient ones, reflected before me in the glass of the show-case.

I wonder now, not only at the portraits, but at all of us assembled here before them. A few moments ago we were simply passers-by, people who had just stepped into the museum from busy streets and stressful jobs, from shopping trips, boring meetings and long train journeys. Most of us had come from fast-moving, frag-mented, information-soaked lives, bringing all the fizz and buzz of the city along with us.

So it takes a while for us to adjust. It's as if we are shy at first, taken aback perhaps less by the portraits than by our sudden silence before them.

The faces we're used to seeing are shiny, hard-edged images with all the seduction of a marketing strategy behind them. These faces, by contrast, look out at us without speculation or guile. They meet our gaze with a degree of candour and openness we're unused to.

Our seeing slows down. Our faces relax.

The longer we linger, the deeper we look.

For all their apparent engagement with worldly affairs, these ancient faces don't appear agitated, distracted or driven by busy-ness. On the contrary, these people appear to be living in the ebb and flow of life without being swayed or seduced by it, dwelling fully and freely within time without being consumed by the fear of running out of it.

And we . . .?

We are no longer a bunch of bystanders.
We have been gathered.
Stilled.
The portraits have recollected us.

*Here actually is a real seer-glance . . . of an eye that is human . . . and beautifully capable of making others see with it.*

Thomas Carlyle, *The Life of John Sterling*

Returning from my trip to India yesterday evening I ate a light snack, unpacked and went straight to bed, but during the night something caused me suddenly to wake up. I sat bolt upright in bed and stared out into shadows of my room and found that nothing around me was recognizable. I could make out the shapes of furniture, the curtains, the pictures on the walls . . . but nothing was registering as "mine". There was simply no flicker of recognition. I had absolutely no idea where I was.

The only thing which kept going through my mind as I sat staring into the darkness was the question: *Do I live here?*

This morning when I woke, everything was recognizable and normal and I knew where I was again.

Apparently, I had briefly slipped my moorings. It was probably a combination of jet lag and culture shock. Perhaps I hadn't yet caught up with myself. I'd been immersed in India for two weeks, living in hill country 500 kilometres south-west of Chennai, where the only sounds were the croaking of frogs by the pond, the voices of *mahouts* calling commands to their elephants as they worked clearing logs, and radio music travelling on the wind from distant tribal villages. So perhaps a temporary disorientation isn't so surprising.

It was strange though, being without that mind which normally keeps me attached to places and things and not recognizing anything as "mine". What surprises me is that I wasn't particularly disturbed by the experience. On the contrary, actually. There was no drama, or panic, just a neutral gaze. I simply sat looking out into openness, and then lay down and went back to sleep.

Still, the memory of waking with that question during the night remains with me.

What does it mean, I wonder?

Do *I* live here?

Do I *live* here?

And who is asking?

The Dutch course doesn't begin until September so I'm trying to learn as much as I can from a textbook and from watching Dutch TV.

Still exhausted and disoriented from my move to Amsterdam, I'm sitting on the sofa this evening, casually zapping from channel to channel, trying to pick out the occasional Dutch word I can understand, when an image suddenly catches my attention. The picture on the screen is that of a woman in a desert. She's climbing over rocks, struggling to keep large sheets of paper from blowing away in the wind. Slowly it becomes evident that she's an artist painting the ruins of an ancient temple.

Next there's an image of her standing in a shelled-out building in a city which could be Beirut. The room in which she stands is open to the skies, the wall behind her, pock-marked by bullets. It's as if she doesn't realize, as if she hasn't noticed how small she is standing in front of that wall.

It's enormously frustrating not being able to understand any of the words, but still I sit spellbound, unable to take my eyes off the screen. I don't know what I'm looking at, and yet something in me is responding. I can't understand it, but I've seen enough to know that this can't be ignored. I know with absolute clarity and certainty: *this I must follow.*

What precisely it is I have to follow, I've no idea. I'm no painter after all. I quickly flick through the pages of the TV guide and manage, through a process of elimination and using the few words I recognize, to locate the programme. I make a note of its title and the name of the artist and resolve to start searching tomorrow to find out everything I can about this woman's life and work.

Cars pass by on the road outside. The neighbour's feet echo on the staircase as he leaves for work. Normally his footsteps are neutral, passing unnoticed. Today, though, I notice them; they resound, bound full of confidence and certainty for the job-world. I sit in silence, going nowhere, feeling alone and monumentally useless.

The little black business suits lie forgotten in a trunk in the attic. Days pass in silence. What if it's a snare? It can't be helped. Comprehensible or not, life takes this course now, knows the way. And I watch; sometimes astonished, sometimes appalled. Feeling the earth shift, solid, strange . . .

I see eventually that there's only one thing to do. So I climb the stairs to the attic, sort and stack boxes, throw away junk, dust and vacuum. Then I make curtains, organise a table and chair, meditation cushions, an icon, some incense, and make a meditation place, a room of my own.

For three weeks I have sat in the attic (in between the shopping, the cleaning, the cooking and the washing up) listening to my heart because there is simply nothing else to be done.

And I keep reminding myself that listening to my heart is *not* doing nothing.

*We see but smallish patches at a time,
and enslaved as we are by the deceptive
present, the synoptic Vision is denied us.*

K.R. Srinivasa Iyengar,
*Sitayana: Epic of the Earth-born*

I've bought the book. The woman I saw on television the other evening was Gerti Bierenbroodspot. She is a Dutch artist and writer; a free-variable, one whose life blazes and dazzles, as disturbing as it is enlightening. The book, *Sign of Taurus*, is about her life, work and travels among the fallen statues and crumbling ruins of deserted cities in the Near East; ancient cities which were once flourishing trading posts along the Silk Road from China and India to the West.

Here she describes a scene in the desert city of Palmyra:

*On the south side of the temple of Bel are two columns of absolute grace and of gigantic proportions. I like the gigantesque . . . Here, I will stand for weeks, to dwell entirely in the columns' presence . . . They speak to me like twin muses: "Paint us, caress us, take us." And so I did.*

49

# Zoe White

Judith Weingarten,
*Bierenbroodspot, Sign of Taurus:*
*The Archaeological Worlds of Gerti Bierenbroodspot*

I'm struck by the expression to "dwell entirely in the columns' presence". It's this dwelling entirely that caught my attention when I saw her on TV the other evening. Bierenbroodspot's act of trust and hospitality in coming to dwell entirely with the enormous columns calls forth an answering hospitality. The pillars give themselves into her embrace, allowing themselves to be transformed in her sight.

This is about more than image-making. The eye of the artist penetrates, reaches in behind the veil, probes beneath the surface appearance of separation. It's a gaze which disturbs; a gaze which is capable of warming a cold earth.

To dwell entirely is a *mutual* in-dwelling. It's not for the faint-hearted. It's not for one who wants to remain untouched or unchanged.

*The longer you work in the same place, the more the secrets of that place emerge. And then, slowly but surely, those secrets appear on your paper. The subject doesn't change; you yourself change.*

Judith Weingarten
Bierenbroodspot, Sign of Taurus:
The Archaeological Worlds of Gerti Bierenbroodspot

None of this helps me with the practicalities of my job search, but this big book feels like the most precious gift. It gives me something of myself back; something familiar in the midst of all the unfamiliarity and frustration of trying to find my way around this new culture.

The *Sign of Taurus* keeps me in touch with a part of myself which I now claim. It may not yet be ready to be fully *lived*, but I have recognized it, and this fact alone gives enormous encouragement.

Dwelling entirely is charged with substance.

I pray for a similar passion.

The man at the job centre is trying to fit me into his computer. He scratches his head and looks at me, weighing up my chances of finding work. He sighs. He's doing his best but it seems that I've got too much experience and too many qualifications for any of the jobs on his computer.

I'd like this to be easy, for his sake as well as my own. I'd like to fit into one of his categories, but he's looking doubtful. A woman over fifty with the wrong mother tongue, looking for work during a recession . . . I can see it's not looking too hopeful.

I decide to put him out of his misery. I tell him I'm willing to take a simple job if it will help me learn the language. His face brightens. "Let's say receptionist then, shall we?" I smile at him, feeling worn out and hopeless.

There's no will anymore to look for jobs. It's not that I'm unwilling to work. I'm more than willing—desperate in fact—to rejoin that passionate engagement with the world that makes money; where there are colleagues to lunch with and an agenda to move me along with purpose and with pace.

So I stare at the Situations Vacant columns, still struggling to look for jobs, unable to quite believe that my life has somehow gone jobless on me.

The capacity to want these vacant situations, the capacity to will them into being, is a capacity I once had, but now all the enthusiastic, energetic, outgoing, team-player words I read here fill my body with weariness. There's nothing wrong with these jobs—they made my life work for a long time—it's just that there's no more substance left to them. They look like masks fallen from a passing carnival parade and I know I have to let them go. My heart's just not in them.

Wise people tell me to enjoy this time of no work. They're right, I know; I should enjoy it. Other people look at me, puzzled, envious, jealous even, that I should be taking such a long . . . what? What to call it? Holiday?

A friend asks: "Have you ever used your training?" I feel like hitting her. I know this is unfair, I know she didn't mean it unkindly, but the question touched a raw nerve. She voiced my own self-doubt and exasperation at what's happening.

Of course I should be using my training. Why don't I have anything to show for it? All that experience, all those qualifications? Why am I not using my talents, doing with my life what people quite clearly see I'm capable of doing? Surely it should all have resulted in something by now; some service, some good for the world. I'm over fifty, for heaven's sake; why am I not picking myself up, pulling myself together and getting my life back on track?

My parents, unable to comprehend it, enquire each week as to my health, suspecting I've come down with some illness too awful to mention. I assure them I'm fine.

Am I fine?

There was a time when I thought I was in the driver's seat, driving, thinking I was going somewhere. Later I had to get into the back seat and let myself be driven. Later still I began to wonder if there was actually a driver. Now I begin to suspect there isn't even a car.

Normal faculties of will, of knowing and planning seem to have been hijacked. Suffering the indignity of deposition, ego rebels, wants to be back in control. But there is nothing left *to* control.

So I sit, small and empty, in the space where the car should be, wondering why I can't get a job, and I wake in the night, tossing and turning in a sweaty panic, certain that this can't possibly be the right path, convinced I've taken a wrong turn and that obviously this way leads to ruin. Why would anyone in their right mind follow it?

I breathe; count my breaths. Slowly, very slowly, sleep returns.

What makes it so disconcerting is that I used to be able to make plans. I used to be able to see ahead, project thoughts and ideas forward, but I seem to have lost this capacity now. It's as though my mind is going flat. This is puzzling and sometimes frightening because I don't recognize myself at all.

I know that all I can really *do* now is learn to turn my face toward the sun and trust the orbit, the new knowing which is directing me.

But then fear arises again along with a kind of wilful activism which springs from panic and from wanting to get my life back on track. I'm not ready to be sitting at home—even if I am doing something purposeful like learning a language. I want to be out doing, earning . . . contributing.

And yet if I'm honest there is also an easeful unfolding. I do sense that work (whatever work is now) is happening through such simple things as the ironing, watering the plants and making the bed. Sometimes I'm also aware of an absorption, like deep rest and an attitude something like non-interference.

What attracts me? A passing shadow, a spider's web, pale sky, leaves blown along the street at dusk . . .

All I know is a sense of having my attention drawn, sometimes to a stone or to a tree . . . it can happen while I'm doing the washing, or writing a letter. Then I become aware of silence absorbing me, like the pull of a tide. Sometimes I feel almost drunk with it, longing to lean into it and move with the ebb and flow of it until I am soaked in that sea, and longing never to be parted from it.

The bell at night wakes me. Who's ringing? My father's death approaching with its attendant terror. Breathe. I can survive this. The father. Our Father . . . Who art *seen*. Apparently. This death could happen any time. The phone could ring. And ring. With its message. Leaving me sweating and lonely in the night. My heart pounds with the dread of it. But I will not shrink from it.

The bell at night. You are alone with that. What will you do?

This death could also be life. Liberation. Creation.

Embarrassing moment at the bank this morning.

Often when trying to speak Dutch, I still get some irritating interference from the French I was in the habit of speaking in Brussels. A French word suddenly pops up in the middle of a Dutch phrase, or else a Dutch word pops up completely out of context simply because it sounds similar to the word I would have used when speaking French. This is what happened today when I went to the bank with some money to deposit.

Instead of telling the cashier I wanted to put this money into my account, I got the French word *compte* mixed up with the Dutch word *kont* and it wasn't until I was leaving the bank that I realized I'd actually told the cashier that I wanted to put this money on my arse!

Some years ago when I was living in Brussels, a mistake such as this would have caused me to wither in shame. Today, though, I noticed I was unphased by it. I even had to smile at myself. I wonder what has changed. Perhaps, after all, I've grown a little in self-acceptance. Maybe it comes from living in so many different cultures and countries. Perhaps my Britishness (my aversion to making a fool of myself) is finally starting to wear out and I'm no longer so invested in protecting an outworn identity.

This incident puts me in mind of the ancient asceticism of *peregrinatio.* Those Celtic monks who exiled themselves from their native country to sojourn as strangers in foreign lands were availing themselves of precisely this kind of identity-toppling experience because they knew the role it could play in the quest for deeper awareness.

I've met Joy several times now. She doesn't come to Europe often. I see her only once every couple of years. She's a Sufi, but she doesn't work for, or from, any particular tradition. Above all she's a healer, but not primarily of the physical body.

Joy speaks what she sees simply, directly and with enormous compassion. Healing (whether of body or spirit) comes as a by-product. The scope of her vision and the crystal clarity of her insight take my breath away.

The personal questions and doubts that I bring to my meetings with her all but disappear because all that is felt in her presence is boundlessness.

As always, after seeing her I write some of her words in my journal.

> *You and I share some things in common . . . we know*
> *our shadows very well. What I didn't know was my*
> *light . . .*
> *You know all your shadows but it's very hard*

*for you to see the other things . . . and you can only
see them if you are quiet. And maybe God has given
you this time of quietness so that you will absolutely
have to see. And it's not ego. You know how to find
ego-voices in your head . . . It's about accepting the
fact that you need to be as passionate about yourself
as you are about everything else . . . If you could see
what a radiantly beautiful creation you are! . . . That's
what is hard to see and that's what you are learning.
Enjoy!*

I'm a long way from being able to appreciate the kind of beauty
in myself that she evidently sees. Despite this, I have to trust her
words because I know her seeing is true. I also know that she is
right; this time of quietness is for learning to see true.

My first spring in Amsterdam. Birdsong outside. Days getting
longer. The sense of absorption still lingering, like perfume,
in the air around me.

Yesterday, quite by chance I came across a book about the Bengali saint Ramakrishna and his followers. As I stood in the shop
reading some extracts, I became aware of the sense of absorption
deepening. As I turned my mind in his direction I sensed a light
pulsing around my heart as if a chord had been struck and the
echoes were reverberating in waves from the centre of me.

I bought the book and am now deeply immersed in the lives of
the people who were Sri Ramakrishna's first followers.

Nineteenth-century India seems a long way from my life here
in Amsterdam, yet—as with the Sign of Taurus—I recognize this
book to be an inspired and inspiring gift. There's so much here
which seems to speak to my experience, particularly what I've been

sensing these last months about the importance of getting out of the driver's seat and letting life live itself through me.

So I welcome all these people and my heart warms within me as I read about them.

Sitting on my cushion in the silence of this Zen retreat, I become conscious of my need to "do it right"; a self which wants to obey; which wants to get acceptance by following the rules; which still needs to please an authority.

And then . . . What is this?

I wait and watch within until the image becomes clearer.

There seem to be mirrors everywhere. They show reflections of myself, and I'm disgusted by what I see. As I watch, the mirrors move closer; they reflect "failure", they reflect "not good enough". I want to turn away because I'm sickened by having myself thrust in front of me in this humiliating way.

But there seems nowhere else to turn. It's as if I'm sitting in the centre of a box room and all the walls are mirrors. So I just have to keep looking, and every direction I look, I'm trying to correct the way I look, but the more I look and try to correct myself, the more self-conscious I become, and the more shame is reflected.

It occurs to me that maybe this is something that's been going on for years now, unconsciously, and that perhaps fighting against these reflections is related to the headaches, which have been getting worse again over recent months.

The only relief I discover in the end seems to come when I turn my attention to my heart. Here there is warmth and here there is absolutely no awareness of the mirrors.

On Friday night I had a dream in which I met a woman with a third eye in the centre of her forehead. When I looked closely into her eyes, I saw that they were an astonishing purple-violet-blue colour. I've never seen eyes of such colour and with so much love in them. I almost cried out with the intensity of that love and when she saw this, she laughed a soft, gentle laugh, and was gone.

Sometime during the night on Sunday, I was woken by the feeling that some kind of force was trying to break out from inside my chest. It was as if this force wanted to explode. Twice it tried to break through and I was so terrified that I think I cried out in fear. Even though I seemed to be asleep I remember feeling awake and fully conscious and I recognized what was happening as something that I had been born for. It was as if I had been waiting for this all my life.

The next day I felt shaky and had to pay extra attention as I cycled to my Dutch lesson. In fact, I was unsure if I could still function in the world of traffic, balancing on two wheels.

I'm still constantly being drawn back to reading about Sri Ramakrishna. The depth of his surrender and devotion to Mother Kali isn't something I understand, but it's clear that in turning my mind in this direction, my heart seems to open, as if to the sun, as if recognising something which has always been calling me.

The mirrors are now magnifying; throwing back outsized judgements and criticisms. All the time they are getting closer and bigger.

"Can you be grateful to the mirrors?" asks the Zen master during my talk with him. "Be grateful. The mirrors are helping you."

Sitting again on my cushion it's surprising how hard it seems at first to actually find any gratitude in relation to these mirrors; to actually get my face to soften and to smile at them. I focus attention on my heart and the muscles around my mouth and eyes, allowing them to relax. Then I notice a more gentle nature revealing itself here. And I see how I've hidden this gentleness from myself. It's almost as though I've withheld it in order to punish someone. Myself?

It's only myself I'm deluding by continuing to withhold these softer eyes.

So I smile in thankfulness.

Immediately the mirrors vanish.

The voice which says *I love you* has been returning. It's not really a voice, just a subtle knowing, beating in time with the rhythm of my heart. And this morning in meditation, I realized that the cells of my body were realigning themselves with this rhythm, so that a subtle change was happening. It's as if I'm slowly becoming the love with which I am loved.

> *Let life live itself through you. This is what will lead you.*
>
> *Trust that what you have done and what you do with your whole heart is enough.*
>
> *Let go of outcomes. Give up trying to follow a formula, give up expectations.*

Today in meditation I was still practising smiling in thankfulness at the mirrors, when all of a sudden they became windows and I could see through them to an openness which was bathed in light.

There are still some attacks of shame sometimes but the feeling of internal pressure from the walls/mirrors has now gone.

What I learn from this is that there was a whole identity based on being wrong and being judged, which was generating brutalising, self-punishing thoughts. This must have gone unnoticed my whole life.

Catch the old thought-habits with good humour. Let them know they have been seen. This is enough.

Yesterday in meditation the image of a door arose. There was a battle between two angels. One wanted to open the door, the other wanted to keep the door closed.

I know that this door is significant.

I also caught myself daydreaming yesterday that someone was coming to give me the message that my father had died.

Meetings with friends seem not to be happening so much now. I keep contact through e-mails occasionally. It's nothing personal, it's just too hard to answer people's concerned and puzzled looks. How to explain that nothing is happening, that nothing is moving? How to explain this being held in abeyance?

I do, though, still come across helpers, co-walkers, guides, perhaps. I meet them mainly through reading. They are people who, for one reason or another, have found themselves leaving the familiar and embarking on an unconventional, perhaps eccentric, course, and there is huge consolation in realizing that my experience—especially this sense of being held in enforced stillness and solitude—has been shared by others.

During the time of the Vietnam war, for example, when Thomas

Merton was challenged about why he was staying in his monastery pursuing his contemplative vocation in the countryside instead of getting involved in the anti-war movement, where he could, arguably, have been doing more good, he replied:

> *I am in the most uncomfortable and unenviable position of waiting without any justification, without a convincing explanation, and without any assurance except that it seems to be what God wants of me and . . . this kind of desperation is what it means for me to be without idols . . .*

> Monica Furlong, *Merton: A Biography*

Similar waiting and desperation was also experienced by Vincent Van Gogh, who described it as being

> *inwardly consumed by a great longing for action, yet [one] does nothing because it is impossible . . . to do anything . . . and then one asks: "My God! Is it for long, is it forever, is it for eternity?*

> Mark Roskill, *The Letters of Vincent Van Gogh*

Pearl Buck, too, expressed deep frustration and puzzlement when she wrote about the ten-year period in her life, between the ages of 25 and 35, which she felt had been wasted:

> *What was I doing in those years? And why didn't I get to work? I see now that I was in a queer submerged state. It was like living in a solitary cell, nothing and no one came in and I seemed unable to communicate*

*with anyone . . . remembering it, I have the feelings of*
*one having spent part of his life in jail.*

Hilary Spurling, *Burying the Bones*

The Zen master's talk today was about the desire which causes us to seek recognition and fulfilment from others and how the human heart, being open to the infinite, can never find complete fulfilment in, or from, other beings. Distorted and disappointed desire can lead to a struggle for power, he says . . . I think of the two angels from my dream. I think of being at the door and knocking and struggling to find a way of opening that door.

He says that the way to freedom has to come through a conversion: a letting go and a falling into the abyss because only then can you be embraced by the emptiness and mystery that is grace. Your true father, he says, is Emptiness! You are the child of Emptiness . . . No, you *are* Emptiness.

The whole talk is a bit much to take in, but I recognize the significance of these words. I think of the night I woke and looked around my room not recognizing anything as belonging to me. That was a moment of pure emptiness.

Seconds pass, minutes and hours tick away. We sit. The bell rings. I stand, walk down the corridor and enter the interview room. The Zen master is sitting on his cushion. I approach him, bow and kneel before him. We are both alert. The air is charged with tension and expectation.

"Behold, I stand at the door and knock," I say.

He shifts his weight slightly on the cushion, barely taking his eyes from mine.

"How do you open the door?" he asks.

I hadn't expected this. I'd been expecting someone else to open it, or at least tell me how to open it. I'd never imagined in my wildest dreams that *I* could open it.

Tears spring into my eyes. "With joy," I say, beaming at him, as the tears slide slowly down my cheeks.

"That's good. Now go back to your cushion," he says as he rings the bell to signal the end of the interview.

I rise, bow and leave the room, elated.

> *. . . contemplation is not vision because it sees*
> *"without seeing" and knows "without knowing"*

Thomas Merton, *New Seeds of Contemplation*

The eyes may have a part to play, but it's clearly not only a question of optics.

The other day I came across this account, written by someone who tragically lost his sight while still a child . . . It describes a new kind of seeing, which he discovered after becoming blind and of which he had previously been totally unaware.

> *Finally . . . I realized that I was looking in the wrong way. . . I was looking too far off, and too much on the surface of things . . . I began to look more closely, not at things but at a world closer to myself . . . instead of clinging to the movement of sight toward the world outside. Immediately, the substance of the universe drew together, redefined and peopled itself anew. I was aware of a radiance emanating from a place I knew nothing about, a place which might as well have been outside me as within . . . I felt indescribable relief, and happiness so great it almost made me laugh . . .*

*Without my eyes light was much more stable than it had been with them. As I remember it, there were no longer the same differences between things lighted brightly, less brightly, or not at all. I saw the whole world in light, existing through it and because of it.*

Jacques Lusseyran, *And There Was Light*

There is a service going on in the main body of the church. Someone tells me in the dream to just go and pray silently by the altar. I'm relieved to be told to do this. It is my deepest desire; just to sit in silence beside the altar. This is where I belong. This is where my whole life has been leading.

But then, looking around me, I suddenly realize that there's no exit up here by the altar, it's a dead end, and this realization ties me up as if in a straitjacket. I panic and struggle, but eventually I see there's nothing to be done except sit here, disarmed, facing the altar; and the sacrifice.

Yet there's concentration somewhere, and comprehension too: the creation of beauty; a soul's radiance. And my heart beats on mindlessly: *my love, my love . . .*

*One may say that the purpose of the universe is to produce great lovers.*

Prem Prakash, *The Yoga of Spiritual Devotion*

Yes, indeed, one *may* say this, but what a pity it is that so few of us do!

I wish I'd heard more people say it. I wish I'd had travelling monks passing by the front door when I was growing up, as Ramakrishna did. I wish I'd seen a stream of *sadhus*, pilgrims and seekers after truth, coming with their songs, their stories and their passion for God.

There should have been hundreds of great lovers coming to our school to show us what being a great lover looked like; to show us there were greater choices, larger visions than those on offer in the careers books, and bigger questions than our teachers ever dreamed of.

I may not have understood them, I may not have gone with them, but at least I would have known that such a life was possible. At least I would have seen that becoming a great lover was one of the options. Apart from the example set by St. Thérèse, the recruiting talk by the woman from the Navy was the biggest vision, the most inspiring thing I got to see.

There should have been a whole host of them. Each year a whirlwind of great lovers should have come spinning past the school gates for us to wonder at. They should have swept us up into ecstatic storms, spun us round and dropped us down again.

Just turning up and radiating would have been enough . . .

Great lovers speak with their lives: *This is what I do. This is what I give my life to. I don't have a CV, I don't have a business card, but becoming a great lover is what it means for me to be alive.*

Where were they?

The problem is, I've always known what to do. But now I don't. There's just this awful doubt. How do I know if this stillness and this waiting isn't just quietism, a kind of inertia, a refusal to engage with the world?

I write to the Zen master to ask his advice.

His reply, when it comes, soothes like a balm:

"We cannot force a way out of stillness . . . You will be very alone in your attitude. I am deeply convinced that most activities are escape. Escape from precisely the point where we discover the painful longing and crying of our heart for fulfilment . . . most activity is an escaping mechanism from this . . ."

I've just written my letters of resignation from the Quakers and from the Buddhist Sangha. I'm not going to Meeting for Worship anymore so it seems the right thing to do. There is really no explanation I can give beyond knowing that it just has to happen, or rather that it has already happened.

Daily meditation continues and I know I will also go on retreats from time to time. However, it's clear that *belonging* to groups and meetings has stopped, and it doesn't seem possible to get it going again. I try to get myself to move again in that direction because those groups have been so much part of my life for the past thirty years. I'm aware of the nourishment they have brought me, but they simply seem not to be happening anymore, so perhaps it's better somehow to admit it. Resigning is a way to make this knowing clear to myself, as much as to others.

Actually, if I'm honest, there has already been something like a warning sound in me for a while now. It's nothing I can explain, just a sense of needing to be alert; something like a smoke detector sounding in the background of consciousness, faint at first, becoming gradually louder and more insistent.

It reminded me of the drill we had to practise during my ground-to-air communications training in the Navy, to prevent a pilot losing consciousness. If you heard a pilot's voice suddenly coming through the ear-phones with slurred speech, burbling nonsense, you had to say one word, over and over and over again. That one word had to get through to the brain, penetrate the delirium and pierce the garbling of one drunk on airlessness: *Oxygen . . ., Oxygen . . ., Oxygen . . ., Oxygen . . ..*

I don't try to explain all this in my resignation letter to the Clerk of Quaker Meeting. I simply say that the only thing I know for sure is that I have to become an attender again. I simply have to go back to what/who I've always been: not doing, just attending. Nothing else. It's the only possible thing now; the only really honest thing.

Notes from another meeting with Joy yesterday:

*Do you see what you are doing as you write? You are trusting yourself to creation. This is not primarily about writing but about living. Trust yourself to the process that is living through you. Trust that it will be revealed. Consecrate not-writing as much as writing. You are learning how to live a surrendered life. This is what it means to get out of the driver's seat; out of the car.*

*You are struggling to stay cramped up in the car, in a self-created universe, but you have glimpsed freedom, you have tasted it. Let go of your resistance. Give up the fear that people will not understand what you write; that people will find fault and criticize. That fear is a way of staying stuck. You are trying to manage the unmanageable. You are trying to work as you have worked before—from understanding. You can no longer work this way.*

Had to stop writing yesterday because of a headache. Spent most of the night awake, sitting up in bed (lying down makes the headache worse), fighting waves of nausea.

There is a memory of spaciousness; or is it anticipation? Hope for simplicity, which I can sense, taste almost. Sometimes it seems to tease, touch, brush past me, stirring longing. To know this—no, not to know it, to *become* it. To write from being . . . rather than from thinking . . . But at the moment writing only seems to take me further away from it.

Or is writing a way to work myself free enough to see it; a way to see to the heart of it? But who knows when I shall have written enough?

Having to stop writing because of headaches is like having to give up my heart's desire.

The apartment is very quiet. Strangely all the panic of a few weeks ago about work and money is gone.

"*Once, this picture was big, really big.*" *Picasso's sweeping gesture indicated a canvas that would have towered above my head. "But that was long ago. I later painted it over with other subjects many times, then cut it to pieces, then painted again. This is all that remains. It is my father."*

David Douglas Duncan, *Picasso's Picassos*

As I was hanging up the washing this morning, a thought arose in my mind. I just stopped what I was doing and said to myself: "This could be it, Zoe; this could be it." Meaning that this could be the rhythm of life now. And then I watched myself packing all my English-teaching books into a box and putting them into storage in the attic. As I watched myself doing it, I was thinking, "This looks final."

Even though I haven't actually done any teaching for years now, I've been reluctant to make the decision to stop. But some bodily knowing apparently recognizes what has to be done and is getting on with doing it, despite myself. I know this has to happen.

While those books remained unpacked I could still imagine there was a life, an old life, to go back to.

I know there are ways to think about this.

I've read in the mystical literature about the great souls who entered the cave, the dark night, the cloud of unknowing . . . and grappled with it. I know that the dissolving of certainties can seem all-consuming and that the impasse can appear to be total.

When I was reading about it, the great unknown looked quite attractive. Living without map or compass, taking only God as guide . . . was exotic, heroic. It looked like a great adventure—when it was happening to someone else!

I didn't know how it would feel actually to *live* it. There was nothing in those books about the job centre, the panic attacks, the migraines or the hot flushes.

I wasn't brought up to be a pioneer. But then again, perhaps no one is.

*I saw everything connected, cellularly connected. I saw air almost like a substance, and I realized— tears came to my eyes—"My goodness, what people*

*call beautiful is really just decay!" When you look at
things, you look at the surface where the dead cells
are. So what we call beautiful is already wilting.
How much greater is the beauty that is underneath
the surface. And the life of the spirit, just before it is
formed, that's when it's most beautiful. To reveal that
beauty became my path.*

Gesshin Prabhasa Dharma
Lenore Friedman,
*Meetings with Remarkable Women –
Buddhist Teachers in America*

Filled with joy and a kind of ecstasy in my sleep, I almost laugh
out loud. Then angels come dressed in astonishing brocade gar-
ments. I try to get a good look at the material because I've never
seen anything quite like it before.

Following the angels is a tall white figure, or perhaps it wasn't
a figure, it could have been a pillar of light. Whatever it was, it was
so tall I couldn't see to the top of it. I understood that I had to go
somewhere with these beings.

Then I had to put a white garment on and as the cloth came
down over my head, I felt as if I was being sucked upwards and
then I began spinning round very fast. It seemed as though I was
conscious and I remember telling myself that I mustn't be afraid,
that I must just surrender. In order to stop myself being frightened
as I was spinning around, I thought of all the people I loved, I called
them to mind, counted and named them.

Then I was in a room with the angels and some other people.
I remember thinking how "normal" everyone seemed considering
the extraordinary circumstances. We were playing some kind of
party game in which you had to guess how many hairs there were

on the head of this one particular red-haired angel—minus one. I picked up some of the angel's hair and as I let it fall through my fingers I realized there were far too many hairs to count so I wrote some arbitrary number down on a piece of paper. Then I wandered around looking at the other people gathered there.

Through a glass panel I could see my father sitting in another room. I waved to him and he acknowledged me a bit stiffly. He hasn't changed, I thought, smiling to myself. He's probably feeling a bit self-conscious here in this room full of angels!

A few years ago, the politician, Pim Fortuyn, was assassinated here in the Netherlands. Now the murder of film-maker Theo van Gogh is followed by arson attacks on mosques and Muslim schools. Adrenaline is in the air; anger, frustration and grief are on the streets. The world's press descends to find out what's happening to this nation, once renowned for its tolerance.

Dutch TV news bulletins this evening reflect images of the Netherlands broadcast from news-desks around Europe. One by one the newsreaders flash onto the screen. From Paris to Moscow and from Oslo to Athens, they are speaking different languages but all reporting the same events. I watch, stunned, as image follows image of formerly quiet suburban Dutch streets now in turmoil; families being evacuated from homes; elite troops storming buildings; marksmen poised on rooftops.

I've lived happily on the continent of Europe for several years. I've made Amsterdam my home, yet now I find myself living in a culture which seems strange—even to itself. The Dutch don't recognize themselves, and if they don't know who they are, where does that leave me? And where did this *they* come from?

I thought I'd become European; thought I'd begun to see us all with the common European eye. But now—now that guns are being fired on streets—the European eye escapes me. At this moment, to be honest, I'm seeing with the eyes of an islander, wondering if there's still time to find a boat and row myself back across the water to the safety of those white cliffs. And I'm disappointed in myself. Crises such as these aren't going to be solved by all of us getting into our boats and rowing off to fortify the shores of our respective lands against each other. This much I *do* see.

It should be obvious by now that our seeing is far from complete. Clearly we still have to look further and more widely, beyond the small circles of identity in and by which we confine and define ourselves (and others). But where to start looking?

Bullets appear to have come from every side; Far Left and Far Right; religious and non-religious; Dutch and non-Dutch. Like spectators at Wimbledon, we follow the ball with synchronized heads as the shots bounce back and forth, wondering how it will end. Is it only the saints and the mystics then who dare take their eye off the ball and risk seeing beyond the competition?

Images continue to flicker on the screen. Politicians plead for calm and dialogue. Police step up arrests. Ominous parallels are drawn: murmurings of *Kristallnacht*. And I crave the distraction of these images, exhausting as they are, because I know what will happen when I switch them off. The air will be charged with the residue of my craving and I'll go to bed as I did on September 11th feeling frightened, wired and helpless, wondering what sort of world I'd wake up to.

So I postpone the moment as long as I can until finally, saturated and stupefied, I reach for the remote and press the button. The screen goes dead.

Looking further and more widely starts here.

More headaches, followed by throwing up and complete physical exhaustion again. I don't seem to be able to write for more than a few days now without migraines arising. No matter how many breaks and holidays I have, as soon as I start writing, the cycle starts all over again. Even when I limit the amount of time I spend writing, my mind gets compulsive, cramped, self-punishing, less playful, less creative.

And then when I finally give myself permission to stop writing for a few days, ideas immediately start to rush in again, creating the urge to get it all down, to empty myself of all the sparks and mushrooming thoughts. And so the cycle begins all over again.

Things have started to move again. Within the space of one week, I've researched the competition, decided on a name, got a new phone and telephone number, put some ads in newspapers, introduced myself to the local vets and distributed some leaflets.

Had it not been for the past year, when I was working as a volunteer at the cat shelter, the idea of starting my own cat-sitting business might never have occurred to me, but working with animals brings me joy and now, apparently, I'm making it my business.

Part of me knows this is the kind of work I have to do now. It gives me the flexibility to work in the way I want to work: organise my own schedule, write when I can, and finally earn a little money to contribute to our expenses.

But above all I know that this is where my heart leads: give the love you can give, where you can give it, and whatever it *looks* like, don't underestimate what can happen through it.

The strange thing is, yesterday I was looking through some notes I'd made at a seminar before leaving Brussels, in which I was brainstorming some ideas for work I might like to do in the future. One of the things I'd written on that list was *work with animals*. I'd completely forgotten this.

The irony is that after struggling so recently with being unemployed, sending out resumés and feeling hopeless, I'm now starting to receive letters of application from unemployed people wanting to come and work for my "company".

I write to a friend from Brussels to tell her what I'm now doing. She writes back: "What a spectacular career change!"

When I tell people what I'm doing they often say they'd also like to do something like this. I don't think they necessarily mean that they want to work with animals specifically. Perhaps what they mean is simply that they'd like to work with their hearts.


It is 3.30am. I must have been woken up by the sounds of the sirens and by car doors being slammed. A fire engine has drawn up outside. In the shadows I can see divers by the side of the canal, getting into wetsuits and preparing breathing apparatus. Police are marking off an area of the road with red and white tape. A few neighbours, woken by the activity, congregate on the pavement as the divers plunge into the canal and disappear beneath the surface, leaving only a stream of bubbles trailing behind them.

Someone sets up a camera on a tripod and walks over to talk to the police. The neighbours stand at a respectful distance, talking softly as they watch the tops of the divers' heads occasionally bobbing up above the surface of the water.

Eventually a body is pulled out of the water and laid on the pavement alongside the canal. The divers climb out of their apparatus and begin to pack up their gear. The police put the body into a body bag. The fire service vans drive off. The neighbours run out of things to say and drift back to their houses. The reporter and the last police car leave the scene. Just one policeman now remains on the empty street, guarding the body.

I continue to stand at the window for a few minutes more and just as I'm about to go back to bed, another car arrives. After a brief talk with the policeman its driver is allowed into the cordoned-off area.

Two more cars arrive and pull up behind the first one, outside a house almost directly opposite the place where the body lies. The doors of the first car open and a bride and groom step out, followed by a cloud of balloons. Then the occupants of the other cars, all in festive dress, spill out into the street, balancing piles of wedding presents in their arms. The air is filled with coloured streamers, the bride is carried over the threshold and everyone disappears laughing and chatting into the light of the party. There are only one or two curious glances thrown towards the policeman; probably no one even notices the body bag on the ground in the shadows.

Soon the street is still again. Only the body, watched over by the policeman, remains. I go back to bed and try to think about what has just happened. Body bags and balloons shouldn't appear together on the same street; shouldn't happen in concert. It is an affront, if you think about it. But actually I found that I *couldn't* think about it. I would have liked some of that red-and-white police tape to string up in my mind so I could shepherd my thoughts into tidy enclosures. Something in me wanted to rewind what I'd just seen as if it were a film, so I could delete some scenes and make it all more *fitting*. But it wasn't a film and I couldn't rewind it. Balloons get everywhere . . . and I had to look.

By morning the policeman and the body are gone. But this happening stays with me. It brings to mind a Chagall painting I once saw called *The Dead Man*. I think it was night time; there was a body lying in a street. Candles had been placed around the body and a woman stood in the street alone, wailing. High up on a rooftop opposite sat the fiddler. You could easily have missed him.

I hear later from a neighbour that a man who lived a few doors down the street committed suicide.

The only thing I could have done—the only thing I *should* have done—was go and place some candles round the body.


*You will come to see that all evolves us.*

Rumi, *Love Poems from God,*
(trans. Daniel Ladinsky)


This quotation reminds me of Julian of Norwich's: *All shall be well . . .*

Small phrases these, but such big *All*s. They remind me of the All I saw on the street the other night.

This is what All means: contradictions, taboos, inconveniences and incorrectnesses. The all-embracing sweep of them.

All is included. The suicide, the policeman, the fiddler, the bride, the groom, the balloons and the wedding guests . . .

Is this what it means, the all-ness of everything?

All is not respectable. But where is the disrespect?

They give me vertigo, these Alls. My mind edges toward them tentatively, about to topple over an edge.

It's here all the time, of course, this compelling, exhilarating edge, but mostly I don't let myself know it. Mostly I collude with the mind, which thinks to manage it, which thinks to rest in more comfortable compartments.

*All* concentrates the eye, if you let it.

*All* brings power into play.


I'm trying to unwind after another intense period of writing. Trying to release the spring of concentration, which has been tightly curled all week. The period of wind-down seems to take so long. Perhaps it's like divers coming back up to the surface from the depths. I seem to have to do it gradually, otherwise the sudden pressure change is too much for the system.

Even as I'm trying to unwind, ideas start to accumulate again.

*You are writing defensively.*

*Allow spaces to remain. Stop trying to think everything.*

*Sell your possessions: let go of the habit of knowing what you're looking at.*

*Enter the play of ambiguity, enjoy it! You are too deeply defended, still standing too far back.*

Another headache attack yesterday, sickness and exhaustion, even though I hadn't been writing all week.

So this morning I return to household chores. *This is hardly enough to keep the mind alive*, I think to myself as I go upstairs with the washing. Perhaps that's the whole point. The mind is having to get out of the way, and sometimes I wonder if writing isn't a struggle to keep it active.

Sometimes I still dream of having a "normal" job, that someone is offering me a way back into the working world I used to be a part of. Then I dream I have lost that job and I wake myself up grieving for it.

*More generous eyes we need*

St Catherine of Sienna, *Love Poems from God,*
(trans. Daniel Ladinsky)

I'm cycling around Amsterdam every day to visit the cats in their homes; feeding and stroking them and cleaning their litter trays. The work is restful because it has no message, no meaning. It takes me into their space: the clear, open space of animal being; cat time.

One of the owners came back from holiday recently and told me that her cat looked so healthy when she returned. She was full of amazement that his fur looked so shiny. I often think that the animals enjoy the time alone as much as the owners enjoy their holiday. Perhaps the owners don't appreciate what peace descends upon these empty houses while they are away.

The song of the blackbird outside sounds clearer, fresher, closer.

What would happen if I really delighted in the beauty all around me?

I might realize that I'm not apart from it.


Some notes from my meeting with Joy last week:

> *You are losing everything in order to get back to basics. . . This is as tough as it gets. You have nothing left to hide behind. You're as free as you've ever been, and as clear. Your career was fine, but you hit a place where what you wanted to accomplish wasn't possible in that way anymore. What you needed as a human being to grow wasn't there. You are bigger than those parameters.*
>
> *For the first time in your whole life, you're living in your passion. What you didn't know is that living in your passion is difficult too.*

(At this point I burst into tears and admit that I'm terrified.)

*But you have to be honest . . . What you have to
ask for is that which supports who you truly are. Look
with different eyes. Don't do anything differently, just
look with different eyes.*

Having done the accounts yesterday, I'm feeling a lot more hopeful. I haven't yet deducted my expenses but still it looks as though the business did better than I expected. I wanted it to be a success, I wanted it to grow, and in just eighteen months it certainly has grown. In fact if the client list continues to grow at this rate I'll have to get some colleagues to help me next year.

Reading some of the stories passed down by the monks in Egypt the other day, it occurred to me that I've perhaps had too stoical a notion of courage.

One story in particular appealed to me. It's narrated by a monk and anchorite by the name of Abba Paphnutius, who is thought to have already been an old man and a venerated monk when he witnessed the dawn of Christian monasticism at the end of the fourth century CE.

Paphnutius' story is alive with detail and ringing with authenticity, as fresh as if it had been written yesterday. It begins with Paphnutius going off into the furthest reaches of the desert to see if he can find any other brother monks living there:

*So I walked four days and four nights without eating
bread or drinking water . . . finally after a number
of days I came upon a cave. When I approached it, I
knocked at the mouth of the cave at midday, but no*

*one answered me. Now I thought to myself, "There is no brother here," but then I saw a brother sitting silently inside. I took hold of his arm and it came off in my hands and disintegrated into dust. I felt his body all over and found that he was clearly dead and had been dead a long time. I looked up and saw a short-sleeved tunic hanging up. When I touched it, it fell apart and turned into dust. I stood up and I prayed, and I took off my robe and wrapped the body in it. I dug with my hands in the earth; I buried him, and I left that place.*

*Now I walked on into the desert and I found another cave. I summoned up my courage and I knocked at the mouth of the cave but no one answered me. I went inside, but did not find anyone. I came out, saying, "This is where a servant of God lives; he will be coming home soon." So I stayed there praying until late in the day and I was reciting Scripture I had learned by heart.*

Paphnutius, *Histories of the Monks of Upper Egypt*
and *The Life of Onnophrius*
(trans. Tim Vivian)

In a footnote, the translator says that the Coptic word used for "courage" in the phrase "I summoned up my courage" actually means "heart". The literal translation of the phrase is "my heart came to me". This invites comparison with the French *cœur* (heart), and the etymology of the English word *courage*.

Just after reading this, I was listening to a radio programme about skylarks. Apparently one of the functions of their song is that of defence. Singing and flying at the same time requires extraordinary strength, and potential predators recognize this. Harriers are less likely to attack those birds displaying such vigour and vitality; the power and courage of the heart-song.

A sudden influx of energy today! Life is flowing again—what a relief! And this sense of vitality is actually no "thing". It's not something new that has been added; it's rather the absence of something old, something like a dam which was stopping the water flowing, and once the water flows again, creation abounds and there is nothing but "life" rushing through.

In my dream last night a man was criticizing something I'd written, humiliating me in public. I was outraged and fiercely defended myself, saying that what I'd written might be simple, but at least it was my truth.

Faced with the ferocity of my defence the man starts to cry. And then he looks around, confused, as if he doesn't understand where his strength has gone.

He can no longer intimidate me. His reign is over.

Standing in the queue at the check-out in the supermarket recently, I overheard the woman in front of me talking about the experience of being made redundant last year. She was telling her friend about the shock of suddenly finding herself unable to pay the mortgage and of her nightmares about being thrown out onto the street. "Anyway", she said, as she was packing her shopping, "it took a lot of faith to get through that experience . . . not *religious* faith, I don't mean . . ."

A few days later I came home and turned on the radio, only to hear a similar comment. "Yes," the person was saying, "I do pray, but not *church* kind of prayer . . ."

I've been reflecting on these *not-religious* and *not-church* remarks. I know I've heard comments like these before. It's as if they've been collecting and hanging in the air around me for quite some time, almost without my noticing. What is meant by this *not-saying*, and what exactly is it that so many people are not saying?

Clearly, it isn't a denial of faith. In fact, the use of "not religious" and "not church" is a way of affirming (albeit negatively) a kind of faith experience, while at the same time registering reluctance to be linked with conventional ways of expressing it.

Perhaps the negative qualifier is simply a way of signaling unwillingness to use words that have lost their link with the experience which gave rise to them.

The more I reflect on it, the more I have to admit a certain sense of solidarity and empathy with the not-sayers. I'm surprised by this because I've always thought of myself as someone who is quite comfortable with traditional faith language (whether western or eastern). But actually (though it's disconcerting to admit it), I know that there is a not-sayer in me, and that this not-sayer may have been singing a quiet refrain under the surface of consciousness for quite some time.

Perhaps my resignation from formal religious groups was, in part, a way of trying to admit the not-sayer. Perhaps the not-sayer in me was telling me to leave the formulas, the code words and the acronyms behind. It's not that traditional expressions were wrong, or bad. It's not that I didn't value them. But there was perhaps another kind of inquiry underway—a need to find my own words— and perhaps the not-sayer just wanted to free me psychologically to plunge into the process.

In fact, I wouldn't be surprised if it was the not-sayer who ignited the passion for this whole contemplative inquiry in the first place.

Browsing in the library today, I pick up a book about Chagall and come across some lines of a poem which Blaise Cendrars wrote in homage to him:

> *Suddenly he paints*
> *He grabs a church and paints with a church*
> *He grabs a cow and paints with a cow*
> *With a sardine*
> *With heads, hands, knives*
> *He paints with a bull's tendon*
> *He paints with all the grubby passions of a little Jew-*
> *ish village*
> *With all the exacerbated sexuality of a Russian province*

Blaise Cendrars
Dix-neuf poèmes élastiques

The inheritance has to be grabbed, seized and painted with. The rules, the creeds, the castes and conditioning, it's all to be grabbed, salvaged, *used*, for life. All is the stuff of creation. All evolves us.

Having no clients, I decide to make today a day of retreat and meditation. Reading a chapter from the Song of Solomon, I pick up a word here, a phrase there:

> *Behold, you are beautiful, my love, behold, you are beautiful!*
> *. . . you are all fair, my love; . . . there is no flaw in you.*

Song of Solomon
4: vv1, 7

As I repeat the words, it's as if they reach into me, turn around, unfold themselves and emerge again . . . *all fair . . . no flaw . . .* and I go on repeating them, unthinking, allowing the truth of them to deepen within; taking them in with my breath . . . *You are beautiful, my love . . . all fair . . . no flaw . . .* until the words *become* me. Until there is no denying it, no division, no separation . . .

*You are all fair . . . There is no flaw . . .*

Until something like a dam breaks and tears begin to flow.

Faith is coming to life
Coming to life is like a lover
Engaging
Igniting
Intoxicating
There are different ways of coming to life
My way is to go around looking at things
What I see is always more than I know

These were the words which came to me this morning as I was waking up. Fully formed they arrived, and sparklingly clear, so I wrote them down and considered them over my toast and marmalade.

It looks like a statement of faith, I thought. There's nothing religious about it, but the words do, nonetheless, have all the hallmarks of St. Paul's "assurance of things hoped for, the conviction of things not seen".

In fact, a sense of assurance and conviction is precisely what came along with the words. There was a definite feeling of flourish and fanfare and, above all, tremendous relief, elation even. It's as if the solution to a much puzzled-over mathematical problem has finally reached me; as though I've arrived at a clearing in a forest, a lighter atmosphere.

This is the first intimation I've had that I'm reaching the end of the book. I know that the book is far from finished, but the sense of relief is undeniable. So what precisely *is* finished?

It's repetitive work, of course. No days off. No status attached. Coming and going each day with my pockets full of front door keys, I talk to the cats as if they are friends, which, of course, they are. There's another reason too. They need to get used to the sound of my voice. If they ever get sick and I have to take them to the vet I want them at least to be able to recognize my voice and hopefully feel less frightened.

We have our rituals. When I arrive, the cats stretch, walk up and down watching me carefully as I prepare their food. Some of them dribble and try to jump up onto the worktop, unable to bear the waiting any longer.

While they eat I clean the litter tray, sweep the floor and change their water. Sometimes they want to play or be cuddled after eating.

But mostly by now they have completely lost interest in me and are content just to wash themselves or settle down to take a nap in the sunshine.

I didn't really need a university education to be doing this work. There's not much thinking attached. Perhaps that's why I'm doing it.

The world doesn't notice this work much. It's not thankless though. The owners notice and the cats definitely notice.

In frustration I wrote to Joy recently that all I was doing was cleaning up shit.

"Yes," she replies, "that's all any one of us is doing."

What I'm learning from cat-sitting is that there are cats all over Amsterdam, sitting quietly in quiet houses, and that even the quiet houses are sitting quietly.

*A lovely forest, full of wonders!*
*In search of food and drink, I gaze around me*
*And lo! my eyes fall on a wandering lion;*
*I look at him steadily—the lion goes quietly away.*
*Divinity expresses itself through the eye.*
*I am the energy of lions,*
*I am the life in all.*

Swami Rama Tirtha
*Scientist and Mahatma –*
*the Life and Teachings of Swami Rama Tirtha*
(trans. Hari Prasad Shastri)

This is the dream in which I am journeyed.
Through the window of my caravan I look out into the woods and see two big cats, sleek like panthers. One has long gray fur with

a wild mane. I'm not afraid of them; on the contrary, I'm utterly captivated by their magnificence.

Then I'm walking through a forest and there's a woman walking alongside me. She has me in hold. From the shoulders down, our bodies are woven into each other, and my arms are threaded through hers. My body seems merged with that of the woman and I am moving quite naturally as one with her. And yet, at the same time, from the neck up, I'm screaming my head off. The body seems totally unaware of any problem while my panic-struck head is yelling in terror.

As I am walking as one with the woman, I notice some other people standing among trees in the wood a little way off. They can see what's happening, and they see I'm desperate. I cry out to them for help, hoping they will come to my rescue, but they continue standing where they are, just looking.

Next I'm in a log cabin. It could be wilderness; pioneer territory. The people I saw in the woods are standing around the sides of the room. *Why didn't you help me?* I ask, but they continue to stand and look on in silence. They aren't hostile; they just don't seem to register my question. It's as if they aren't able to understand my fear. They are standing impassively, as witnesses only.

The woman is sitting at a table in front of me, signing a document. It could be a covenant; a contract perhaps? After she has signed the document, she turns it round so I can read it. She points to some words underneath her signature. She wants me to understand: it's not her name she is pointing to, it's her profession. I look where she is pointing and read: *Lifeguard*. Then I look up into her face. She is gazing at me and her eyes are full of compassion.

I was apprehended from the outset. Once I'd glimpsed the wild cats it was a foregone conclusion. Once I'd caught sight of their beauty, their power and their grace, I went where they went. No question.

I've decided to write to Joy to ask her advice about the headaches. I'm desperate. I've tried everything I can think of and I simply can't go on like this anymore. I can't write and I can't *not* write. There's so much passion for writing, so much anguish and exhaustion when I have to stop . . . and now the headaches are combined with about ten hot flushes per day and I've simply come to the end of trying to understand and manage it all.

The doctors have only been able to suggest painkillers and/or anti-depressants. Some of the painkillers one doctor prescribed caused my stomach to bleed, which meant I had to go to hospital for a very uncomfortable and completely unnecessary endoscopy. Alternative therapies, homeopathic remedies and herbs have all helped somewhat, but the headaches always come back eventually.

I know I'm a perfectionist; I know I don't dare to write badly. I've tried not writing; I've tried to carry on writing despite the headaches. I've tried to rest; I've prayed. And now I seem to have come to the end of the line. I need help and Joy is the only person I can think of. She doesn't come to Europe any longer, but perhaps she can help via e-mail.

Lying awake observing the rising of a panic attack one night this week a question suddenly occurred to me: *What if this life leaves no trace?* I lay there considering the possibility: What if everything I've worked for and everything I've struggled to become in this life simply vanishes? As it surely will.

Following this I felt a peace so profound that it seemed to go deeper than the muscles and nerves of my physical body. It was an instant of pure emptiness and utter rest and immediately I fell asleep.

Joy has replied. She thinks that the physical problems such as headaches are symptoms; indicators of the real issue. The issue is not about writing. It is more about my *response* to writing. Writing triggers stressful thoughts, which in turn trigger migraines.

It boils down to taking responsibility for ourselves, she says, and not allowing other people's actions to determine how we feel.

> *The night of the panic attack, you gave up your illusions for a while and achieved peace. That is what you need to do. Your authority has never come from your writing, but from your soul. Your writing comes from your soul experience, not your illusions.*
>
> *My suggestion would be to make a painting, a collage or a sculpture that represents writing . . . include whatever comes up and do not make it from intellect. Create the image from your gut and heart. Don't try to understand what you are making. In doing this what you are doing is creating outside the problems inside, to get answers . . .*
>
> *The second part of the exercise is to "live" with what you have created and observe it. No judgement, negative or positive. Write down any observations you have. Let yourself not know anything.*

The phone rings. My father has collapsed and been taken into hospital. I have to get myself over to the UK.

My two colleagues are taking over my cat-clients while I'm gone.

> *. . . order comes out of chaos, again and again. You let the order come out of the chaos. Don't try to arrange it . . . It is very difficult to explain, because it's not*

*fully formed in my mind; it does not come into the rational consciousness properly.*

Bede Griffiths,
*A Human Search; Bede Griffiths Reflects on his Life*
(ed. John Swindells)

Now back in Amsterdam again following my trip to the UK. My father is still in hospital, still having trouble breathing, but is now stable. The doctors are looking into the possibility of an operation, in which case he will be moved to London.

My main concern though was really to help my mother through the initial shock and get support systems in place so she can cope at home alone.

I've got another flight to the UK booked in two weeks' time; meanwhile I return to life here: cat-clients, continuing with the paintings and talking with my mother every day on the phone.

As I explore the images I've painted in response to Joy's suggestion, I notice an accompanying voice which berates me; a heaviness and a sense of loss weighing me down . . .

> *Keep up your observations with the painting . . . create an image of the Voice, again not in judgement but as an observation . . . putting a "face" and an identity upon it is taking it out of the shadows . . . It will test you by trying to hide, giving you a false identity . . . you must pull your mind down to your heart, for the heart cannot be fooled . . .*

*The question the Divine asks us over and over
again is "What do you want?"*

Apart from continuing with the paintings, I've been thinking
about what Joy wrote in her last e-mail: *The question the Divine
asks us over and over again is "What do you want?"*

What springs immediately to mind is the example of Sri
Ramakrishna. I've been meditating on him a lot recently and feel
him to be a source of great nourishment. Such merging with the
Divine as I feel in his life brings tears to my eyes. To be totally dis-
solved in and by that same surrender, to be alight with it, radiate it,
draw others into it . . . This is the deepest desire of my heart, and, I
believe, my life's work.

I'm surprised by the clarity and conviction which accompanies
these words as I write them.

Still phoning my mother, and the hospital in London, every day,
speaking to nurses and sometimes to my father if he is well
enough to get to the phone. They seem reluctant to give me any
information about if or when they are going to operate.

Another e-mail from Joy has come:

> *The illusions, projections and assumptions are not,
> and never were, real but the pain you caused your-
> self is, and was. Now you have an awareness and the
> capacity to change. These things are not unconscious
> now; they have an identity, and names, and are recog-
> nizable. Now you must initiate the new beginning of
> what You want! You, my dear Zoe, are the book the*

*Divine is writing. The "book" you are going to write/
are writing is a healing of many wrongs and miscon-
ceptions . . . and an awakening of another stage of
consciousness. Don't get discouraged. Overwhelm is
one way we stay stuck.*

*Trust yourself! This is not impossible. Laughter is
a great defence!*

My mobile rings. It is my mother: "Daddy has gone."
For a second my mind can't comprehend it.

Gone where? I think.

As I cycle back through the woods to the station to catch the train to Amsterdam, the trees alone absorb the shock and witness the wailing.

There have been so many farewells these past two years as his heart condition has worsened. At each parting I know he has been wondering (as I too have been wondering) if this would be the final one.

So that one, two weeks ago in England, as he stood by the door of his hospital room waving goodbye to my mother and to me, *was* the final one.

His wave was gentle, his eyes full of love, but I could let myself see it, let myself *feel* it at a distance only . . .

. . . only on parting.

The hardest bit today was choosing hymns for the memorial service. The one I chose to close the service is "God is working His purpose out".

Somehow I know that this is what's happening. This lifetime, all lifetimes, with their qualities, idiosyncrasies, achievements and misunderstandings are but small aspects of one enormous purpose getting worked out.

This Sunday, which falls between my father's death and his cremation, is Pentecost. I decide to go to the local Quaker Meeting for Worship. The weather continues to be warm and sunny. The skies are a brilliant blue and I walk to the Meeting House, breathing in the fragrance of lilac blossoms.

After lunch I lie down in the park by the lake in the shade of a great flowering chestnut tree. Bees buzz, children play and laugh, the whole afternoon is like a balm, soothing my raw nerves and frayed emotions.

Suddenly, as I'm walking back through the park, the screeching of a bird breaks the calm. I look up and catch sight of a crow with a fledgling in its beak. The crow is being hotly pursued by the parents of the young one and in a flash, the pastoral scene and the peace of the afternoon are shattered.

Being already in a state of shock and exhaustion from the past days' happenings, there is no defence. I bury my face in my hands as a wave of horror sweeps through me. At the same time I know that this is life in the wild. I know that what I've seen is as natural as the fragrance of lilac and the buzzing of bees.

I can't say exactly *what* I saw in that moment. I only know I saw something that I deeply did not want to see. Before I knew it, I had seen it. Something in me felt rent by the seeing of it and it's too late now to pretend I didn't see it.

It turns out that there was more to be seen.

A few months after the death of my father, I began to do some research into the family history, particularly that of his mother's family. It was almost as though some force at my back was powering the search. I spent hours scrolling through records on the internet, working late into the night until finally I found what I had apparently been looking for. My grandmother is listed as being one year old during the 1901 England Census and there are four other children. *Four!* I stare at the screen in disbelief. She had four elder brothers.

My father had often spoken of his aunts, (his mother's younger sisters) but he had never mentioned any uncles. But here they are: four brothers; my father's uncles. How can four boys just have disappeared? Can it be a mistake? No. One boy could perhaps be wrongly listed, but *four* boys can't be a mistake. I look again. This must be true. Here they are, in black and white, my grandmother's four brothers, aged four, six, eight and ten. I check with my mother. No, she says, she never heard my father speak of any uncles. Could my father have had four uncles and never known about them?

Feeling as though I'm opening the windows and doors of a house which has been shut up for generations, I search the next census to see if I can find later records of these boys. I check the births, deaths and marriages. Here I find something. One of the brothers got married in the 1920s, but the other three seem to have disappeared from the records completely.

There is only one explanation. Somewhere between 1914 and 1918, along with so many others, three boys left home one day and did not come back. These boys, my great-uncles, became the disappeared. The Lost. Perhaps the one surviving brother, the one who married, became estranged from the family. Who knows?

My grandmother grew up to marry one of the few men who survived the Battle of the Somme. Then she herself gave birth to two boys, the first of whom was my father. They all had to get on with life, of course, as best they could. But the question must still have remained, for all of them: How to love again?

So I carefully write their names and dates of birth on the family tree I have drawn: Charles, Russell, Donald and Percy. Three of them were already dead some years before my father's birth but they still deserve to be remembered in the land of the living.

During my next visit to my mother in the UK, I suddenly feel a heaviness gathering over my eyes and above my heart and it becomes clear that there has to be a symbolic burial. I have nothing to bury but the family tree which I have been carrying with me. The sun is shining this morning and I know I have to do it today because the grief is getting heavier, and it has to be done here in England. I will not tell my mother. She is still getting over the recent scattering of my father's ashes.

Knowing I want to read something at the burial I go to a charity shop in town and search through the second-hand poetry books. One book falls open at a Robert Frost poem about a meeting with deer in a forest, and as I read it, the tenderness in the poem finds an answering tenderness in me; a love for those lost boys. I know I have to include this in my ritual. I also find a Wilfred Owen poem.

Then, back at my parents' house, I go out into the garage to look for something of my father's to bury with the family tree. I ask the air: "What shall I use?" And immediately my eye falls on a pottery mug lying in a box with some old garden tools. I have never seen this mug before. It has my father's name on one side, and on the other side an engraving of a deer's head with antlers. The symbolism combines perfectly with the Robert Frost poem. I shall take this.

So I roll up the family tree, place it inside the mug, pack a small trowel and set off for the graveyard. When I get there I sit for a while on the wooden bench with the sun's warmth on my back, thinking again of the hymn we sang at my father's funeral about the purpose being worked out . . .

Thankfully I am alone in the graveyard. I begin by speaking the boys' names out loud. I begin to say: "I am sorry . . . I am so, *so* sorry . . ." And then the grief in my heart cracks open.

These words are my words, yet I'm aware that they are also not just mine. They are my father's words, my grandparents' words and they are spoken now because for nearly a hundred years they were unspeakable.

The tragedy and the mess of it all is way too huge to be anyone's *fault*, but still someone has to say sorry.

When I have calmed down a bit I read the Owen poem: "The Sentry". And then I take the family tree in the mug to a quiet corner of the graveyard, telling the boys that I am their great-niece and that they are now being remembered and buried with their nephew, my father, whom they never knew and who never knew them.

And then I start to dig a hole in the ground, but it's difficult to dig; there are too many roots and my hands are soon slippery with mud, which makes me think of the dirt and mud of the trenches—the awful thud and crack and splinter and shock of war, and a family's frantic forgetting. If they went through all that, I think, surely I can manage to dig a small hole here in a quiet village graveyard. But the trowel is too small and there is no strength left in my hands.

Eventually I manage to scrape enough of the mud away to bury the mug and I cover the place with earth and leaves. Then, after wiping the mud from my hands, I stand reading the Robert Frost poem, "Two Look at Two".

The poem describes two people out walking in a silent forest. It is late afternoon, almost evening. Coming to some barbed wire and a wall, the people, thinking they have come to the end of their walk, are almost ready to bid the woods goodnight and turn back. But then unexpectedly, two animals appear, a doe followed by a buck.

It's a silent meeting, a simple seeing across crumbling walls from one field into another; a meeting of intimacy and courage which extends beyond all endings and beginnings, beyond all fear of what is faced, and of what may be met in the looking.

The task is complete. I walk back to the bench and watch the sun begin to set behind the winter branches. Then I walk back towards town with a quieter love in my heart, leaving the dead to rest in peace.

When pain arises now (be it physical pain or the mental anguish of shame-filled, self-judging thoughts), I'm seeing it and simply returning to the mantra:

*You are beautiful my love, you are beautiful*
*Behold you are all fair; there is no flaw in you*

I let the words fill me; feel them *absorb* me.

If I wake with a headache, I repeat the mantra, let the truth of it seep deeply into my being and go on repeating it all night if necessary. Slowly, very slowly, my body begins to relax and warmth returns to my hands and feet.

Gradually, I learn to see the pain with more distance and to realize that it will pass. This is sanity. Pain comes and goes, like a cloud. I take a couple of paracetamol if necessary and then I watch until it passes.

Then one day I see not only that it passes but also that pain no longer has the power to define me. Scars may remain, but suffering can be left behind.

The more this awareness is confirmed in me, the less energy is available for pain-generation. Habits of suffering have established their pathways over many years, perhaps over generations. They are not going to go away overnight. But the thoughts which cause pain are now recognized as they arise. I acknowledge them and turn my attention to the larger life; the all-being with which I am one.

Slowly my life starts to witness to an alternative way of being; a lighter, more easeful way. All-being breathes a kind of warmth through me. Little by little I allow myself to soften and delight, to blend and flow with life again until I am vibrant and strong, like the skylark, singing and flying, higher and higher in the bright, summer air.

This doesn't necessarily mean the end of pain. If it comes back temporarily, I know it can be immersed again in the mantra and that *essentially* I am undiminished and untouched by it. It's not a question of pain. It is a question of choice: Truth or Illusion? The recognition of choice is the spaciousness I have longed for, and the gift which the migraines have brought me.

Pain may come back, but I know now that I'm no longer in servitude to it.

The process of healing which Joy had walked me through brought me back to what I had already discovered unconsciously as a child at school drawing my picture of Home. Once she had helped me identify the dis-eased, restless selves which seemed to have me in their grip, I could see that I wasn't stuck in my conundrum. I didn't have to be confined by the mind's categories. I could step back, as I'd done in childhood, pick up my viewer and align myself with a larger vision and a more whole, healed gaze.

What I'd not realized was how deeply entrenched and debilitating a belief in victimhood could become. I had not seen the extent to which self-judging and self-brutalizing thoughts were operating undetected. Neither did I realize how, once having established themselves, they not only undermined creative expression, but ultimately made it all but impossible to function normally.

Once I had seen all this, the choice was simple: I could go on finding someone or something else to blame for the conundrum, or I could drop it. I could go on waiting, disempowered, hoping that someone else would make the choice for me, or I could make it for myself: come into alignment with my heart's seeing and surrender everything to a larger being . . .

Perhaps this is part of what Vincent van Gogh meant about becoming "one of the watchers not one of the sleepers".

This morning it became clear to me that what I've been doing is less about writing, and more about collecting metaphors.

The writing process wasn't so much a raid on the inarticulate as a raid on the formulaic. There was, apparently, that in me which was compelled to search out metaphors which moved me, which seemed to have life in them and which stirred life in me.

The gathering of metaphors helped me unlearn my beliefs. Metaphors functioned as centralizing symbols; wove themselves into mantras and helped me bring the power of the heart into play.

Metaphors were like pieces of a jigsaw. Magpie-like I spied them, swooped down on them, picked them up and flew with them. Back in my nest, I gave myself to the arrangement of them, wondering at their colour, their form and sparkle. I loved to behold them.

Metaphors alone didn't have the power to bring me back to life, but the ardour with which I gave myself to the ransacking, the swooping, the arranging and beholding, did.

All is now seen, and all is loved.

The magpie too is loved.

Getting ready for bed the other evening, I noticed more lightness than usual. It wasn't that the room was lighter, neither was it anything I had acquired. In fact, the lightness was only really recognizable by the *absence* of something. There were no anxieties; there was nothing at all to worry about. I was simply spacious and untroubled, like the surface of a lake, and the only thing I had to do, my only *job,* was to reflect light.

The immediacy of this experience faded overnight, but the knowing of that self which is clear, naturally sourced, replenished and sustained remains with me. It is here, all the time in fact, but when the mind is busy with its habitual occupations, this more subtle field of consciousness simply goes unnoticed. I know now that I am not apart from it; in fact, I now realize that there is nothing apart from it.

Last night the perfume-seller
gave me a rose
and I remembered
how you once came
and said

*I come in peace*

I could have told you then
that we would end up
living together
but I thought part of you
was still outside me then
and that dreams
were only for dreaming

Now it is dawn

there is a rose called Peace

and the fragrance is everywhere

# III

# Review

*In a way, ours is the older method, somewhat like that of Darwin on the* Beagle. *He was called a "naturalist". He wanted to see everything, rocks and flora and fauna; marine and terrestrial. We came to envy this Darwin on his sailing ship . . . Faced with all things he cannot hurry . . . Out of long long consideration of the parts, he emerged with a sense of the whole . . . It was the pace that made the difference . . . The results are bound up with the pace.*

John Steinbeck, *The Log from the Sea of Cortez*

As I read back through what has been written here, it looks as though contemplation has woven itself like a silver thread through a varied terrain of countries, cultures, occupations and relationships. Despite the intricacy and complexity, two aspects of contemplation seem to emerge quite clearly.

The first of these is a natural and spontaneous sense which I call simply "wondering". The second is more focused and had to be learned. This I call "remembering".

By wondering, I mean either wondering *about* something, or *just wondering*. It's an easeful, reflective kind of musing; a savouring and delighting, which can be happening anywhere, at any time: while in the shower, standing in a queue in the supermarket, doing the ironing or taking the dog for a walk. Wondering is the mind in free-range mode. It's just what happens when the motor of the mind is allowed to idle.

As a child, I was probably more naturally attuned to wondering and maybe drew on it more routinely. Wondering about the natural world around us is, after all, one of the primary ways in which we learn. It is this reflective, wondering capacity which allows us to be absorbed and playfully immersed in the world around us. There is an element of curiosity in it; one thing leads to another, surprises arise, spaces open out. It's the way quirky connections and new discoveries are made.

As I grew older and came increasingly under the influence of family and social conditioning, materialistic concerns started to dominate. It was then that a more tightly focused thinking mind began to take over. This mind, busy with study, work and projecting identity was necessary for functioning as an adult and for "getting on" in the world. The capacity for wondering then took a back seat but it never got totally forgotten, neither did it ever get entirely lost. On the contrary, writing was my way of continuing to value it and draw on it. For most of my life, wondering was a passion, and writing was my way of mining the seam of that passion.

Then came a time when the other aspect of contemplation began to unfold. This, the remembering phase of contemplative inquiry, came into play when I began to see through the illusion of the pain-filled persona and set off on the way back to sanity.

The word *remembering* as I use it here doesn't refer to remembering something from the past. Rather, it refers to the recalling of my true nature, the nature of being itself.

When I'm taking a photograph and notice that I'm standing in my own light I shift my position slightly to allow more light through. In the same way, remembering is a slight shift in mental positioning, which may be done with the help of a short prayer or mantra, so as to allow the light of a wider, more spacious perspective into awareness.

When I first wrote to Joy asking for help, all I could see was suffering; I thought I *was* that suffering. What I could *not* see was the self-concept which was causing the suffering. I was convinced that writing was the problem. But Joy was right: it wasn't about writing; the suffering was arising from my attachment to a false identity. I just needed to remember to adjust my position.

What Joy pointed out was that I had the capacity to take a step back. The suffering self (the self I *thought* I was) could be witnessed. I was not compelled to identify with it, and I was not bound to suffer it. I could, in other words, remember my true self, which is infinite, boundless consciousness.

I had not realized how deep my attachment to this false identity had become, neither had I seen how chronic was my addiction to toxic thoughts. The painting exercises Joy had me do were ways of helping me see the self-sabotaging thoughts more clearly because until I was conscious of them I had no way of freeing myself from the pain they were causing me.

Once I'd learned to recognize the way these troubling thoughts arose in consciousness (with their attendant physical symptoms of tension and headache) I could stop resisting them, or fighting them and actually *use* them to remind me to return to the mantra and a more easeful, open awareness.

Remembering was a more intense and concentrated aspect of contemplation than wondering. Unlike my instinctive capacity for wondering, remembering had to be consciously practised. What had to be learned might actually better be described as a process of unlearning, because nothing new had to be acquired. It was more a process of releasing my hold on what was not true.

While Joy initiated the remembering phase of contemplation, the ground had already been prepared. The twenty years I'd spent with the Quakers and the ten years practising Zen meditation had helped quieten the mind and had already taught me to become aware of my thoughts. So the process was already partially established.

I've no doubt that I wouldn't have come to this remembering aspect of contemplation without being pushed into it by the migraines. The pain-filled, ego-driven self—the one I had believed myself to be—was too deeply entrenched for me ever to have recognized it or released it naturally. As long as my job, health and strength had lasted, I would have continued to try to live with the old self-concept, and this second aspect of contemplation might never have unfolded.

The remembering process took time and patience; it didn't happen overnight. But gradually, as the years passed, the practice became more habitual and the migraines diminished in intensity and frequency. The encouragement I then felt, in turn, helped make remembering easier. Eventually, I began enjoying the process so much that I actually looked forward to getting a headache, not from any perverse enjoyment of pain, but rather because of the pleasure of plunging again into the mantra and returning to peace.

The process which began with Joy continued to deepen subsequently with other teachers. It wasn't long before I discovered Advaita Vedanta: the Upanishadic vision and science of unity, as transmitted via the Direct Path. These teachings were similar to what I'd already learned in that they also shifted the focus of the gaze from the suffering to the position of the witness and encouraged me to remember to step back, as it were, from the illusory self and ask: Who is the one seeing all this?

Although the Advaita teachings used slightly different language, and although this process happened via self-inquiry rather than with a mantra, the effect was the same. To the extent that I was no longer bound up with the dramas of an individual persona (either suffering them myself, or projecting them out onto others) I noticed a lightening of the body-mind and a wider, more expansive field of awareness. The more I learned to identify with this awareness, rather than with the mind's comings and goings, the more the background happiness and spaciousness simply came to the fore.

The pain of the migraines had forced me to see that the self I thought I was could no longer be sustained. The individual identity I'd built for myself was unsustainable because it wasn't sourced in truth. There has been a therapeutic effect. I'm no longer suffering the heaviness caused by habitual, self-defeating thoughts and it's now possible to write without migraines.

However, the exploration which has been the subject of this book doesn't stop with the personal. The snapshots captured and collected in the Picturing section hint at a broader scene, an infinitely more varied and far-reaching landscape. Words like "wondering" and "remembering" may serve as points of orientation, but they are markers only. The *experience* of contemplation is dynamic; it is a power whose ramifications reach way beyond the confines of "cure".

This power, at least as I experienced it, seemed to be fundamentally connected with nature and with community. Contemplation appears to have brought with it an intuitive, sub-conscious knowing that I am not apart from *all,* and that this *all* is the fabric out of which I too am made.

The pictures may have shifted and slid around as I wrote them: a rocking-boat here, an artist there, a gecko, a portrait, a magpie, a lake . . . But whether I was picking up plums in the convent grounds; out walking the North Yorkshire moors or celebrating Easter in the south of France, nature seems always to have been bringing me back to my senses. The whole environment was living and breathing; always, everywhere, being revealed to itself. Contemplation was always absorbing me, and everything served to draw me deeper into this absorption.

The whole contemplative inquiry has in fact now come to have something of the scope and substance of natural history. Just as the natural historian looks into plants, minerals, stars, insects or fossils, so I was drawn to look into this not-apart-ness until I *realized* it.

Nature provided the raw materials, gave me hints and clues about where to look. And nature seems to have compelled me to look in the same way as a plant is compelled to turn towards the source of light.

Consciousness had to expand, it's as simple as that. I couldn't have continued to function without realizing the allness of everything. Headaches alerted me. I just had to adapt, develop strengths I didn't know I had.

As it works for the individual, so it works for the collective. Standing up and walking on two feet rather than continuing to crawl around on all fours also made sense; common, evolutionary sense. It was the way we could see further and more widely. Eventually there came a time when our senses told us: straighten up, broaden the horizon of seeing, or die.

Under long, close observation, seeing becomes honed, connections come to light. As one comes into deeper alignment with nature's purposes, sooner or later it is apparent that a nebula is not an object in itself, but simply a stage in star development and that caterpillars and butterflies are not two distinct beings, but actually the same animal.

Sooner or later there will also come a time when we will look at ourselves and be astonished and say: "How could we ever have thought we beings were separate one from another?"

*

I didn't realize contemplation as a power that *travels,* until I came into contact with the company arising. This was the company, already mentioned in the Preview, which arose in arbitrary, ad hoc ways, mainly through reading.

Communities of one sort or another had always been an important part of my life. However, after moving to the Netherlands, finding myself in a new relationship, going through culture shock, the menopause and migraines, I found it impossible to continue to participate in communities and groups as I'd once done. Even if I did

108

manage to get to meetings, I found that the effort needed to interact with other people socially and sustain membership over a period of time was more than I could manage.

Perhaps it was precisely *because* I suddenly found myself unable to rely on forms of community I'd once been accustomed to that I became more sensitive to the effect of this other company which now assembled itself around me.

Many, though not all, of the people who made up this company were creative artists of one kind or another. They were people who trusted their own criteria of truth and beauty and were humble enough to refuse to stifle the lyrical motives which guided them.

I appreciated all of them as inspiring individuals, but I certainly didn't think I had much to *do* with them. They came from widely divergent disciplines, professions and periods of history. Unlike the communities I'd been used to, we didn't share common interests, cultures, backgrounds or belief systems. These were exceptional people. They were talented. I, on the other hand, tended towards the ordinary. My life was mundane and conventional. I liked structure, organization, planning and control. I wasn't an artist; there were no artists in my family, and I certainly wasn't brought up to be a risk-taker.

While I may have doubted that I had much in common with these people, I couldn't deny that I was responding to them. Whether it was Gerti Bierenbroodspot painting her columns in the desert, or Sri Ramakrishna in his temple in India making offerings to Mother Kali, their lives *registered* in me as the beat of a drum or the ringing of a bell registers. Even if they had long since left their bodies, these lives *carried*, and I found myself moving to the pulse of them.

Eventually I came to see that varied as their professions were, the *vocation* was one and the same. It had nothing to do with the specifics of their work; it had to do with the heartfelt way in which they *gave* themselves. Self-surrender was central to the calling these people shared. Whether they were artists, writers, musicians or monks, their work involved bringing themselves into alignment with their heart's seeing and their soul's intelligence, even if it meant risking anguish and ridicule.

To come into contact with this company was to experience its transmitting power. I didn't understand this power; I *felt* it because I was ringing with it. Despite my fears and self-doubts, this is the company which inspired me to begin to take writing seriously.

Unlike my previous experiences of community, this wasn't about joining anything. Indeed, there was no thing to join. The power of this company was an en-*cour*-aging power. Quite simply, these people dared me to take heart. Despite our differences, *taking heart* was the life of our common being. The company and the call were one. I was already in and of it by virtue of having been moved by it. This, for me, became the essence of the contemplative vocation. To register the heart-sound was to be drawn into communion and to be made one.

*

The more I reflected on my experience of this company arising, the more I began to appreciate the true nature of another company; one which sprang up many centuries ago through the transmission of a similar power. This was the company of Christian renunciates which arose in Egypt during the third and fourth centuries in response to Jesus' invitation to *go, sell what you possess . . . give to the poor, and . . . follow me.* These were the people whose lives gave rise to what has come to be known as Christian monasticism in the West, and the Hesychast tradition of the Eastern Orthodox Church.

Theirs was a movement full of ardour and audacity, which caught light and spread like wildfire across great swathes of land, from the Nile in Egypt, to regions as far apart as Palestine, Persia and the Arabian peninsula.

The monastic tradition is sometimes regarded today as a private calling, withdrawn from the world and having little social relevance, but in its initial stages at least the movement was far from being withdrawn or private. On the contrary, the lives of these renunciates had enormous social power and huge political ramifications.

The majority of those who caught the beat and breathtaking heat of Jesus' invitation had been living on the margins of society. Many of them were poverty-stricken farmers crippled by Roman tax burdens or people evading military service. Some were criminals; many were misfits. Most of them would have been offensive to polite Roman society and some of them wielded an authority which made even battle-hardened Roman centurions tremble.

Jesus' vision *struck* them. They *got* the power and picked up the pulse of it. The invitation to sell your possessions included, but went further than the doing of good deeds. It went further even than the keeping of the commandments. It was a call to freedom. His life had sounded and they were *re*-sounding. No longer bound by the conditioning and languages of Empire, they were transmitting in the vernacular, and they were unstoppable.

Whether they lived in abandoned tombs in the desert or remained in the family home in cities or in suburbs, the renunciate's vows of poverty and chastity could not have sent a clearer signal: the Roman Empire (which valued wealth and dynastic continuity) no longer had the power to define them.

Marginalized and brutalized they may have been, but it was not too late! They didn't have to earn their freedom, or wait to inherit it. Poor as they were, they could still live sonorous lives; they could still step out of the boat, take responsibility for their own souls and become what He was: a liberty-taker.

*

A few nights ago I dreamed that I went back to the convent for a visit. The sisters are gathering around me, all radiating good health

111

and beaming happiness. I'm surprised that none of them looks older than forty. There's laughter and sunlight in the room and I'm filled with joy to be back among these sisters whom I love.

Then someone brings out a document; it's a kind of record of the brief period I spent at the convent. My photo is here, together with some comments written by the Mother Superior: her impressions of my first few weeks. I move closer to try to read what she wrote, but still I can't manage to decipher the writing. So I reach out my hand, pick up the page and quite calmly tear off pieces of the report and put them into my mouth. It's only as I'm chewing the pieces of paper that I realize I probably shouldn't have done this because it isn't my property, but by the time I see what I'm doing, it's too late. I've swallowed it. Then I wake up.

For many years I felt like a failure for having left the convent. I feared that I'd given up too easily on my vocation, chosen ordinary, secular life above God and disappointed the sisters with whom I'd hoped to establish my belonging.

Now though, freed from its cultural underpinnings and belief systems, contemplation appears to be emerging more clearly and more universally. I see now that it was never primarily about institution, occupation or profession; it was never tied to specific realms, either of imagination or belief. Contemplation was always drawing me into a more essential belonging and ever since leaving the convent I've been chewing it over, taking it more deeply into myself.

I may have left the convent, but the vocation—my heart coming to me—was never abandoned. *All* was pointing to it; and *all* turned out to be a power greater than my power to resist. Creative capacities can be blocked, temporarily shut down through adverse childhood experiences, shocks, trauma, poverty or neglect. But the capacity—our common human capacity—for heart-felt seeing can never be blocked.

The company arising is the same today as it was in the fourth century and for thousands of years before. The invitation is a perennial one: to become a Friend of God, to turn towards the sun, take with you what you can carry: a prayer, a poem, a mantra, a psalm and chew on it. Let it flow in your blood and beat in your heart. Become a great lover. Give the rest away.

*Thy words were found, and I ate them*
*And thy words became to me a joy*
*and the delight of my heart*

Jer. 15:16

# Acknowledgements

Although I wasn't aware of it when giving this book its title, the *Book of the Heart* has roots which go down a long way. Almost as long as people have been writing, the book (whether in the form of parchment, wax tablet or codex) has been visualized as a container for that which is laid upon the heart. I would like to express my sincere thanks to Eric Jager for his fascinating scholarly study, *The Book of the Heart,* which I came upon by chance as I was preparing to publish, and which helped this present book to recognize its lineage.

It has been a real pleasure and privilege to work with an intercontinental team on the production of this book. Thanks to my wonderful editors in the UK and the USA: Isabel Tucker and Elise Yoder, your fresh eyes and sensitive, insightful comments did much to encourage and revive me when I was flagging. Thanks to Tosca Lindeboom in the Netherlands for bringing your sensitivity and creative imagination to the cover design and to Michelle Lovi in Australia for steering the manuscript so carefully and capably through the final stages of typesetting and proofreading. Your combined creativity, professionalism and technical know-how gave this book wings. It has been a delight to collaborate with you all.

I would like to express my gratitude to those who were willing to read the manuscript and offer me their comments especially Von Keairns, Tilden Edwards and Virginia Ramey Mollenkott. Thank you all for your candid reflections, your moral support, your generosity and your friendship.

To Pia Keiding, my deepest gratitude for your courage in accompanying me through the borderlands many years ago and for introducing me to the late Joy Messick, whose crystal clear insight made such a profound and lasting impression on me. I am thankful to you both for your sweet-spirited presence on this pilgrimage.

I am indebted to the Buddhist teachers referred to collectively in this book as "the Zen master". They are Rev. Daizui MacPhillamy, MOBC; Fr AMA Samy SJ and Prof. dr. Ton Lathouwers. Deep gratitude also goes to Rupert Spira and to Mooji Baba, contemporary teachers of the non-dual, Advaita Vedanta tradition, for transmitting Self-awareness so authentically and so simply.

Sincere thanks go to my parents: to my late father who grew the sweet peas in the garden and made kites for me to fly, and to my mother, now in her 90s, who cooked the Sunday roasts and kept my childhood drawings safe. Without you, I, much less this book, would never have seen the beautiful light of day.

Rescued from the shelter and, sadly, no longer living with us here on earth, Yva, our cat companion, didn't have the best start in life, but her small, persistent steps in trust and her enormous courage in keeping loving company with us was perhaps the most inspiring gift of all. A more enduring and poignant example of heartfelt presence would be hard to imagine.

To all the sisters at the convent, past and present: a wordless, timeless gratitude. This book is, perhaps, my belated answer to Sister Madelene's question about prayer.

Finally, thanks to Meindert, my partner, for your generosity in keeping food in the cupboards and a roof over our heads for many years while this book got itself written. Thank you for your love, for your perceptive comments on the manuscript, your commitment to journeying alongside me, and for your frequent reminders that "All shall be well".

# Notes

Carlyle, Thomas. *The Life of John Sterling* II, vi, London, 1871, p. 137

Cendrars, Blaise. *Dix-neuf poèmes élastiques,* Au Sans Pareil, Paris, 1919

Duncan, David Douglas. *Picasso's Picassos* (Abridged), Ballantine Books, New York, 1968, p. 41

Friedman, Lenore. *Meetings with Remarkable Women – Buddhist Teachers in America,* Shambhala, 2000, p. 275

Furlong, Monica. *Merton: A Biography,* Collins, 1980, p. 303

Griffiths, Bede. *A Human Search; Bede Griffiths Reflects on his Life,* Edited by John Swindells, Burns and Oates, 1997, p. 98

Hugh of Saint-Cher (d. 1263) quoted in *The Book of the Heart,* Eric Jager, University of Chicago Press, 2000, p. 59

Iyengar, K.R. Srinivasa. *Sitayana: Epic of the Earth-born,* Samata Books, Madras, 1987, v.782, p. 264

Lusseyran, Jacques. *And There Was Light,* Translated by Elizabeth R. Cameron, New World Library, Novato, California, 2014, pp. 11–13

Merton, Thomas. *New Seeds of Contemplation,* Abbey of Gethsemani, 1961, p. 1

Orwell, George. *Coming up for Air,* Victor Gollancz, 1939, pp. 164–65

Paphnutius. *Histories of the Monks of Upper Egypt* and *The Life of Onnophrius*, Translated by Tim Vivian, Cistercian Studies Series number 140, Cistercian Publications, Michigan, 1993, p. 146

Prakash, Prem. *The Yoga of Spiritual Devotion*, Inner Traditions International and Bear & Company, Rochester, Vermont, 1998, p. 46

Rabia of Basra. *Love Poems from God*, Translated by Daniel Ladinsky, Penguin Compass, New York, 2002, p. 9

Rama Tirtha, Swami. *Scientist and Mahatma – the Life and Teachings of Swami Rama Tirtha,* Translated by Hari Prasad Shastri. Shanti Sadan, London, 2006, p. 53

Robinson, Roxana. *Georgia O'Keeffe,* Bloomsbury, 1989, pp. 166, 256, 484

Rumi. *Love Poems from God,* Translated by Daniel Ladinsky. Penguin Compass, New York, 2002, p. 65

St Catherine of Sienna. *Love Poems from God*, Translated by Daniel Ladinsky. Penguin Compass, New York, 2002, p. 201

Spurling, Hilary. *Burying the Bones,* Profile Books, 2011, p. 178

Steinbeck, John. *The Log from the Sea of Cortez,* Pan, 1951, p. 123

van Gogh, Vincent. *The Letters of Vincent Van Gogh,* Edited by Mark Roskill, Flamingo, 2000, pp. 125, 180

Vivekananda, Swami. *Inspired Talks* (Revised Edition), Ramakrish-na-Vivekananda Center, New York, 1987, pp. 104–05

Weingarten, Judith. *Bierenbroodspot, Sign of Taurus – The Archae-ological Worlds of Gerti Bierenbroodspot,* Waanders Publishers, Zwolle, 1998, pp. 59, 62

All biblical quotations are taken from the Revised Standard Version of the Bible, Oxford University Press, London, 1952

Printed in Great Britain
by Amazon